American public administration

public affairs and administration
(editor: James S. Bowman)
vol. 3

Garland reference library
of social science
vol. 169

the public affairs and administration series

James S. Bowman, editor
Florida State University

1. career planning, development, and management
    an annotated bibliography
        Jonathan P. West

2. professional ethics
    an annotated bibliography and resource guide
        James S. Bowman
        Frederick A. Elliston
        Paula Lockhart

3. American public administration
    a bibliographical guide to the literature
        Gerald E. Caiden
        Richard A. Loverd
        Thomas J. Pavlak
        Lynn F. Sipe
        Molly M. Wong

4. public administration in rural areas and small
    jurisdictions
        a guide to the literature
            Beth Walter Honadle

5. comparative public administration
    an annotated bibliography
        Mark W. Huddleston

American public administration a bibliographical guide to the literature

Gerald E. Caiden
Richard A. Loverd
Thomas J. Pavlak
Lynn F. Sipe
Molly M. Wong

Preface by Warren Bennis

Garland Publishing, Inc. · New York & London
1983

Library of Congress Cataloging in Publication Data
Main entry under title:

American public administration.

   (Public affairs and administration series ; 3)
(Garland reference library of social science ; v. 169)
   Includes index.
   1. Public administration—Bibliography.   2. Public
administration—United States—Bibliography.   3. United
States—Politics and government—Bibliography.
4. Bibliography—Bibliography—Public Administration.
I. Caiden, Gerald E.   II. Series.   III. Series: Garland
reference library of social science; v. 169.
Z7164.A2A53   1983   [JF1351]   016.35'0000973   82-49151
ISBN 0-8240-9152-3

Cover design by Laurence Walczak

Printed on acid-free, 250-year-life paper
Manufactured in the United States of America

contents

v

series foreword

The twentieth century has seen public administration come of age as a field of study and practice. This decade, in fact, marks the one hundredth anniversary of the profession. As a result of the dramatic growth in government, and the accompanying information explosion, many individuals—managers, academicians and their students, researchers—in organizations feel that they do not have ready access to important information. In an increasingly complex world, more and more people need published material to help solve problems.

The scope of the field and the lack of a comprehensive information system has frustrated users, disseminators, and generators of knowledge in public administration. While there have been some initiatives in recent years, the documentation and control of the literature have been generally neglected. Indeed, major gaps in the development of the literature, the bibliographic structure of the discipline, have evolved.

Garland Publishing, Inc., has inaugurated the present series as an authoritative guide to information sources in public administration. It seeks to consolidate the gains made in the growth and maturation of the profession.

The Series consists of three tiers:
1. core volumes keyed to the major subfields in public administration such as personnel management, public budgeting, and intergovernmental relations;
2. bibliographies focusing on substantive areas of administration such as community health; and
3. titles on topical issues in the profession.

Each book will be compiled by one or more specialists in the area. The authors—practitioners and scholars—are selected in open competition from across the country. They design their work to include an introductory essay, a wide variety of biblio-

graphic materials, and, where appropriate, an information resource section. Thus each contribution in the collection
provides a systematic basis for managers and researchers
to make informed judgments in the course of their work.

Since no single volume can adequately encompass such a
broad, interdisciplinary subject, the Series is intended as a
continuous project that will incorporate new bodies of literature as needed. The titles in preparation represent the initial
building blocks in an operating information system for public
affairs and administration. As an open-ended endeavor, it is
hoped that not only will the Series serve to summarize knowledge in the field but also will contribute to its advancement.

This collection of book-length bibliographies is the product
of considerable collaboration on the part of many people. Special appreciation is extended to the editors and staff of Garland Publishing, Inc., to the individual contributors in the Public
Affairs and Administration Series, and to the anonymous re-
viewers of each of the volumes. Inquiries should be made to
the Series Editor.

James S. Bowman
Tallahassee

preface

Gerald Caiden and his associates have taken what may be considered a difficult project—an annotated bibliography—essentially what could be a boring and banal task—and gone way beyond, perhaps even their own, certainly my expectations. They have created a book that virtually all students and practitioners—not only students and practitioners of *public* administration—should own.

Typically, one contributes to the state of knowledge in one of three ways: (1) by advancing theory or methodology, (2) by synthesizing and reconceptualizing, and (3) by codifying and consolidating. While the authors make no claims beyond the third of these objectives—i.e., developing a damned good bibliography for the field of public administration—they have actually charted the boundaries of the field, adumbrated the "faults" and strengths of the field, and shown where the significant work has been done and, inevitably, where more seminal work is required.

Put differently, the authors began with a relatively modest and circumscribed task: to take the "blooming, buzzing" welter of books, journals, official documents, reference works and God-knows-what-else and, with arguable but eminently fair criteria, selected out of that messy and erratic potpourri the essential and seminal works. Now *that's* a contribution that should ease the "information-overload" anxiety that seems to be endemic to fields such as public administration.

In fact, as I read over the manuscript, I began to realize that this book, with only a few exceptions, could be equally useful to the overlapping fields of business administration and related fields in the administrative sciences. Gerald Caiden and his colleagues have accomplished what so many other similar undertakings have failed to: a description of the field, its predominant intellectual landmarks, what's essential to know and, even more importantly, where and how to find out about what is not known. By so doing they have created a work which will ultimately become required reading for all of us whose lives are touched by the execution of public policy. Given the vitality of the field and the increased recognition it has received within the centennial of its origin, we can all look forward to future editions.

Warren Bennis
University of Southern California

introduction

The literature of a given field of knowledge is normally relied upon to record significant new findings, to summarize current developments and to reinterpret the basic structure and guidelines of an area of inquiry. When the available literature is relatively small, it is possible to know fairly easily and quickly almost everything that is worth knowing, to keep abreast of the state of the art, and to make personal evaluations on what is significant, enduring and valuable. But when, as is now the case in most fields, the available literature is vast and expanding in all directions, it is impossible to be knowledgeable about every aspect, to be *au courant* of developments, and to know what should be known. It is enough just to keep up with one's specialization. For the rest, reliance is placed on general overviews which sacrifice depth for breadth and selected guides which make judgments about value and relevance. An encyclopedic bibliography of everything that has ever been written about a field does not discriminate between what is and what is not central and is altogether too overwhelming to be much use. A select instrument is needed that winnows out of what authorities consider the crucial core of the field and provides newcomers the essence of the state of the art and indicates where they can find the most recent discoveries.

This volume is intended to provide such an instrument for students of American public administration. The field has grown so large, particularly over the last decade, that even specialists have difficulty keeping up to date with their own sub-fields. In the course of our professional pursuits as teachers, researchers and librarians, we had developed our own guides to the discipline. For this book, we have pooled our efforts and carefully scrutinized our material to design a guide that would be modest in size yet comprehensive in coverage. Drafts of the manuscript were circulated to practitioners and students while each section was tested on different audiences to gauge reactions and gain feedback. Given such a broad and disparate literature, we knew that there would never be universal agreement and that it would be impossible to satisfy everyone who felt that his or her work had not been given sufficient attention. Hard choices had to be made if the task was to be manageable, and the decision to include or exclude any particular contribution had to be based on a concensus of the authors.

Our aim was to suggest a basic minimum library that could be used for both instructional and research purposes. It would contain readily available sources in print or for which permission to reproduce could still be obtained from the copyright holders so as to provide a guide for students and professional researchers in the field of American public administration. Early on, it was realized that because of their sheer bulk, two sources would have to be excluded: (1) official documents such as public laws and annual reports of public agencies for which readers will have to rely on government information services, and (2) articles published in professional, trade and academic journals. What remains, then, is basic reference material, leading journals, and books which permit access to the literature, including government documents and journals.

Measured by the volume of material available, it would seem that the study of American public administration has never been healthier. More publishers than ever before seem to be willing to launch new works in the area. As a result, more outlets for publication exist. In 1982, newcomers to the subject could choose from over 30 basic texts whereas less than a decade previously they had only a handful. Likewise, instead of a few journals, several new periodicals appear every year while the size and number of issues of established journals have expanded. This publication boom has accompanied two decades of rapid growth in postgraduate studies, training in public management, research on the public sector, and international technology transfer. A new readership had opened up with the enlargement of the government and a significant shift from private to public employment between 1960 and 1980. The number of public laws, services, organizations, accounts and officials had all increased dramatically, so much so that toward the end of this expansionist period, a discernible reaction against further growth was evidenced at the ballot box.

Similar growth periods in the study of public administration had occurred before, most noticeably when the United States had been involved in war and postwar reconstruction, when economic growth and industrialization had necessitated heavy public investment, and when social misery had demanded public relief. But this latest boom had both a quantitative and a qualitative difference about it. The weight of public opinion had decidedly shifted from being anti-statist to pro-statist. The administrative state was fully accepted some decades after its logic had been accepted in other industrialized societies. The contrast is best seen in the constitutional support given to governmental initiatives in the post-Eisenhower years as against the constitutional defeat of a number of Roosevelt's New Deal programs. The administrative state, not the church or the family or business, had become the primary instrument for shaping American society, and public administration had become the focus for political activity. To get something done, one had to go through government, public officials and the bureaucracy.

The protrusion of the administrative state has led to several reinterpretations of the scope of public administration. At first, attention was concentrated on the institutional arrangements whereby governments executed their decisions. Then, following the publication of Woodrow Wilson's seminal essay "The Study of Administration" in 1887, the focus switched to more efficient ways of conducting public business. The Great Depression redirected attention away from *how* governments should operate to *what* they should be doing, and the quality of public decision-making. By the early 1960's, President Kennedy was referring to public administration as the management of industrial society, which took it beyond the confines of government into the realm of public policy, social engineering and inter-sectorial relations. At its widest interpretation, public administration would concern itself with the public ramifica-

tions of social intercourse, certainly all public affairs, an inclu-
sionary concept that would exclude only specific private
affairs.

The mainstream of the literature, however, has been reluctant to go this far. It has been unwilling to depart from its
traditional base in the administrative or managerial aspects of
the public sector defined in strictly institutional, i.e., governmental, terms. Consequently burgeoning studies of public policy have been kept separate or distinct although in recent
years increasing attempts are being made to fuse or integrate
public policy with public management. What this means is that
one can find under the rubric of public administration specula-
tions about the future of civilization and office manuals for
budding executives and virtually anything relevant to the conduct of public affairs in between. We have chosen to stick
closely to the core of the field with occasional forays into the
wider territory of government affairs.

Even so, American public administration contains large
areas of subject matter which stand on their own. Many of
these specializations will be dealt with in companion volumes
to this bibliographical series. Some overlap is inevitable and
unavoidable and probably beneficial. This bibliography is by way
of an overview and reference is made to leading works in the
field, irrespective of specific specialization. We have, however,
omitted specialized public sector professions such as police
and law enforcement, fire prevention and public safety, public
health and medical practice, social welfare, public education
and teaching, librarianship, diplomatic service, and military
service, as well as public lawyers, accountants, economists,
agronomists and the like whose work in the public sector may
include a substantial administrative component. These areas,
however, may be efficiently accessed by consulting the indices
in Chapter Two.

Minimally, the generic constituents of American public administration theory and practice include:

- the ideological roots of public institutions including social contract, federalism, separation of powers, representative
  government, civil rights

- theories of public administration; administrative norms
- contextual influences on public administration
- the role of public administration in society
- the functions of administration
- the history of the public sector
- institutional arrangements of public service delivery, forms and structures, administrative organization
- public and administrative law, public controls, and administrative discretion
- behavior of government organizations and public officials, codes of conduct
- relationships between public organizations and between them and other social organizations
- relations between public officials and the people
- citizens' images and opinions of the public sector and officials' attitudes toward the public
- public sector productivity and performance—measurement and evaluation
- public planning and forecasting
- policy formulation and implementation
- management of government organizations, including leadership and supervision
- public finance and budgeting, accounting and auditing
- public personnel management and labor relations
- professional development: education and training for civil service
- public enterprise
- comparative public administration
- the anthropology and sociology of the field
- biographies of civil servants
- research methods
- public information, accessibility

This list guided us in formulating the bibliography and largely determined what was excluded as being beyond its scope.

Chapter One gives a fuller explanation of how we constructed the boundaries around the bibliography. Ten compelling reasons are advanced to show why the scope of American public administration differs from that of another country. Chapter One also explains that because everyone seemingly has his or her own ideas of what constitutes public administration as a social function, profession, and discipline, there will inevitably be disagreements as to what should be included. Those who concentrate on the *administrative* or managerial side of the study draw the boundaries much narrower than those who concentrate on the *public* or societal side of the study. We are caught in the middle, but claim to be more representative of mainstream public administration than those who would confine it to strictly managerial concerns or those who would expand it to cover the whole gamut of public affairs.

Nonetheless we have found it difficult to maintain a uniformly consistent position. In Chapter Two, an annotated directory of abstracts, indexes, and continuing bibliographies, for instance, there was an irresistible urge to include all relevant sources that should be known to researchers. In contrast, the directory of relevant journals in Chapter Three had to be more exclusionary as there are hundreds of periodicals that occasionally include articles relevant to public administration. We decided to confine the list only to journals where one is reasonably likely to find articles on public affairs and administration. Even then, a second cut was made to omit occasional series and many magazines focused solely on American politics and government, particularly at state and county level.

The greatest difficulty occurred in Chapter Four, which is devoted to the leading books. The annual output is so large that selection had to be stringent. Several designs were tried, none of which proved as satisfactory as the final decision to classify them into six separate sections. One section consists of popular classics at least twenty years old, another three sections cover as fully as possible major textbooks, anthologies, and bibliographies, case studies and workbooks respectively, a fifth section lists the most frequently cited current books, and a sixth section provides more specialized volumes. This division minimized duplication and overlapping and avoided a miscellaneous list of books that did not conveniently fit elsewhere. Reluctantly, we omitted books central to other related disciplines but not strictly within the boundaries drawn. To explain and justify the choices made, we considered turning the whole chapter into an evaluative bibliography. While that might satisfy our consciences, it would further prejudice our readers who should arrive at their own evaluations. The task was difficult enough without proceeding to the more controversial stage of evaluating the literature of a whole field of study.

In producing this selected bibliography, we are conscious of several weaknesses in the current literature, especially in administrative history, public law, public enterprise and theory, to mention just a few. We are also aware that in other areas, such as public personnel management and public finance, the same unoriginal material keeps appearing over and over again. We feel that much needs to be done to grasp the full complexities of the issues in public administration. For instance, we would like to see more attempts made to explore the implications of the dependence of the bureaucracy upon a political process which is increasingly characterized by (a) high degrees of symbolic manipulation, (b) self-aggrandizing power centers in a context of high ecological and technological interdependence, and (c) cultural hostility to collective action. By revealing the richness of current literature, we hope to stimulate our readers to explore these and other issues and to advance the state of the art in what is increasingly a crucial field of study for the betterment of humanity.

Los Angeles and	Gerald Caiden	Richard Loverd
Pittsburgh	Thomas Pavlak	Lynn Sipe
October 1982		Molly Wong

1.
the scope of
American public administration

1. THE SCOPE OF AMERICAN
PUBLIC ADMINISTRATION

Gerald E. Caiden

The contemporary study of public administration is relatively young. It dates back barely two hundred years to the bureaucratic transformation of the modern nation state when a clear distinction was made between the private property of rulers and the public property of the state. At that time an administrative apparatus independent of the personage of state rulers was clearly identifiable. It was separate and distinct from any other social organization. This public bureaucracy has since evolved into the administrative state, that is, the deliberate use of public administration to transform social conditions and reshape society according to prevailing conceptions of progress. It is seen as an active and decidedly partial participant in public affairs pushing and pulling other social institutions in accordance with its authoritative version of public policy. The scope of public administration is determined in large part by the intervention of the administrative state in public affairs and the range of activities conducted by the public bureaucracy at supranational as well as national levels.

Because the path that the administrative state takes is full of surprises--there is no telling what it will do next or what it will be asked to do--the study of public administration may lag behind events. Indeed, the administrative state was well established long before it attracted the serious attention of the academic community. This is particularly true of the United States (a) where it arrived later than in Western Europe and the British Dominions, (b) where ideologically it has been resisted ever since and only begrudgingly accepted in practice, and (c) where Big Government has had to compete fiercely with politically dominant Big Business. Looking back, it is now difficult to comprehend: first, that only in the early 1940's was a professional society formed to "advance the science, processes, and art of public administration"; second, that the first identifiable graduate schools in public administration

and the first professorial chairs were established in the
1920's; and third, that the first serious research studies were
undertaken in the 1900's. This contrasts with European experience where public administration had been recognized as a professional field of study and an intellectual challenge comparable to law at least a century before that. Until well
into the present century, American scholars and practitioners
had to travel to Europe to study the theory and practice of
public administration.

American public administration developed independently
and it remains quite idiosyncratic to the country and its
people. Attempts to export its models have rarely been successful just as efforts to import foreign ideas have rarely
succeeded at home. Public administration was not subsumed
by law as in Europe or integrated into the study of government
as in the British Commonwealth. At the outset, both law and
political science (the American equivalent to the study of
government in Great Britain) laid claims to it. Relatively
early, however, it broke away from both, thanks largely to
the strong and persuasive arguments made by Woodrow Wilson and
Frank Goodnow at the turn of the century that the study of
public administration should be separate from the study of
government and the study of law. That independent tradition
has persisted. American public administration is like no
other, and the body of literature that now encompasses it
stands separate.

THE DISTINCTIVE NATURE OF AMERICAN PUBLIC ADMINISTRATION

The scope of American public administration is distinct
in at least ten ways. First, in contrast to the European
tradition, it excludes public law. Public administration is
not seen as the exercise of public law. Law is seen as part
of the judiciary and the judicial system, and under the American doctrine of the separation of powers it is identified with
the judicial branch of government, not the executive branch.
Until recently, whenever the two overlapped, public administration gave way to the superior claims of the legal profession.
Now, with public and administrative law becoming increasingly
important to the practice of government, public administration
is reaching out into judicial dimensions which the legal profession has been reluctant to explore. Nonetheless, public
administration falls far short of the strong legal inclusion
found in other countries where public law and public administration are indistinguishable.

Second, in contrast to the British tradition, it has excluded, until relatively recently, considerations of the ends of

government and the uses of public office. Public administration has not been seen as the exercise of power. Public power has been seen as part of the study of political science and in the dichotomy that was propounded by Wilson and Goodnow the study of politics and uses made of public office were separated from the study of administration. Whenever the two overlapped, public administration yielded in this case to political science. With the acceptance of the administrative state and the emergence of Big Government, the processes of government can no longer be separated from the purposes to which they are put. Public administration has come now to include the objectives as well as the practices of public management. It has also been reaching out into policy and public interest dimensions which political scientists have been reluctant to explore. Nonetheless, there is still much diffidence, if not downright reluctance, to go beyond the dimensions of the management of public organizations. American public administration falls far short of the strong political inclusion found in other countries where public affairs have never distinguished between policy and administration and where the ends of government have never been separated from the means. Only recently in American public administration has it been realized that the two are (and probably always have been) fused and only recently have strong ideological differences emerged over the role of the administrative state in modern society.

Third, the generalist approach to the administration of public affairs has not been embraced in the United States to the extent that it has been elsewhere. The generalist tradition of the British administrative culture and the stress placed on intellectuality among European bureaucratic elites have provided an inclusive administrative profession to which other public management specialists have been subordinate. In contrast, the early emergence of strong professions in this country before the acceptance of a managerial profession (let alone the notion of a superior administrative cadre in the public bureaucracy) has fragmented the public sector into many rival concerns, few of which have accepted the superior imposition of a generalist administrative elite. Consequently, American public administration has been more of a residual than an inclusive entity. The armed forces and the management of defense have always been excluded, so too have the police and the management of justice, fire fighters, social workers, and teachers as well as members of the traditional professions (law, medicine, religion, higher education) employed in the public sector. These independent professions have jealously guarded their territory against intrusions from a generalist profession of public administrator. Since they were on the scene first, public administration has been reluctant to con-

front them and has tried to devise an amicable modus vivendi
for peaceful coexistence. From a strictly logical point of
view, the historical and political boundaries drawn between
them make little sense. Compared with other countries, American public administration is less inclusory of public sector
activities.

Fourth, the business community has been powerful in the
United States and its influence over the public sector has
probably been stronger than elsewhere. Many activities directly provided by the public bureaucracy in other countries
are provided in the United States by the private sector or
the significant third sector betwixt business and government,
either directly or under contract with public authorities.
Although part of the administrative state, they are not considered part of public administration; that is, scholars and
practitioners have been reluctant to include them in their
domains. On the one hand, this voluntary abstention has left
significant gaps in the study of public administration which
are now being filled hesitantly and inadequately. On the other
hand, the blurred boundaries among the public, private, and
third sectors have also opened up opportunities for the study
of their interface which have been seized possibly to a greater
extent than elsewhere. The same is probably true of intergovernmental administrative arrangements because of the
blurred boundaries and jurisdictions among federal, state,
regional, local, and community agencies in the United States.

Public administration in this country, fifth, is pragmatic, not ideological. The major concern has been to discover
what works best in the public interest, construed in purely
American terms in the light of prevailing conditions; ration-
alizations, justifications, and theoretical underpinnings
have come afterwards. Yet this practical emphasis in American
public administration should not be allowed to obscure its
strong political roots in liberal democracy and the dominance
of political principles over administrative practice and convenience. Democratic liberal values are paramount in American
public management theory and practice. They are the lifeblood
of the public bureaucracy. They are the unwritten premise
on which the administrative state is expected to conduct itself.
Since this is so well understood, American public administration has not felt the need to articulate its norms as much as
other countries where the conduct of the state is subject to
strong ideological differences and continuous political bargaining and shifting compromises.

Sixth, there really is no American public administration.
It is a theoretical construct. Like Weber's ideal bureaucracy,
it exists nowhere. It is a hybrid of common ideas and practices
which have been abstracted from what exists. It is not a com-

plete picture of reality, nor is it a photograph of specific
circumstances. The United States is too diverse. Administrative arrangements and practices differ from one place to another, sometimes quite remarkably. In dealing with public
administration as it really is, one experiences continual
culture shock because experience contrasts so much with expecta-
tion. There are no common frames of reference; every office
seems to be a law to itself, choosing within limits those
practices which best suit itself. It is this variety that
confuses and forces a level of abstraction that nowhere con-
forms exactly with reality. As a result, much in the study
of public management is what should be rather than what is,
and most is analytical not descriptive.

Next, because of constant change in public administration,
history has little contemporary meaning. Historical analysis
has little relevance to the present. In any case, administrators are so caught up with the present that they have little
time for the past and little interest in having the past re-
constructed for them. In brief, there is relatively little
administrative history and, as the expense of holding archives
for purely historical interest is rarely justifiable, the
possibility of reconstructing the past diminishes with every
passing year. The task is so daunting that there are few
volunteers and precious little market. As a result, there is
little historical continuity and many things are continually
being rediscovered because often the left hand does not know
what the right is doing (or has done). Anyway, Americans are
not too proud of their administrative past nor of uncovering
administrative skeletons that should remain buried. What is
done is done. Only the present counts and making the future
better counts even more. Public administration in this country
looks forward not back.

Eighth, few figures dominate public administration in the
United States. Other countries can point to their administrative heroes, those few individuals who dominated the public
bureaucracy in their day or revamped it in their own image
which lasted for an appreciable period after them. Not so
here. Americans do not indulge in much historical veneration,
least of all public administrators. One of the few exceptions
is Robert Moses who dominated New York government for decades,
but his legacy has almost vanished and his reputation has not
lasted. The same applies for the scholastic domain where no
figure has emerged comparable in status to a Max Weber or a
Maynard Keynes. Leonard White exercised some authority for a
period as did Dwight Waldo, but the only Nobel Prize recipient
has been Herbert Simon, much of whose pathfinding work was done
in public administration, but since the 1950's he has not been
associated with the field. If there have been no giants, there

have been many persons of commendable stature who between them
have made the development of the field a cooperative venture.

Ninth, the absence of an intellectual colossus, lateness
in arriving on the American scene, and the tendency to frag-
mentation, have all caused public administration to fight for
its place in the sun. It is frequently overshadowed by such
more powerful disciplines as law, political science, and
business administration which primarily serve other constitu-
encies. These rivals claim that public administration does
not exist or that if it does, it is a minor part of something
else (usually themselves), that to be anything more than a
minor or subdiscipline, it will have to demonstrate more than
it has a proper intellectual or theoretical base, a clear and
unquestionable core, well-defined boundaries, and a logically
consistent whole. In brief, it should have a distinct and
commonly accepted paradigm in order to be accepted as a fully
fledged member of the academic community. Outside the United
States, public administration does not suffer such intellectual
indignity nor react with such an intellectual inferiority complex. In this nation, public administration is continually
forced to reaffirm itself, to justify its existence and to protect itself from takeover bids. It is continually searching
for its soul, for its *raison d'etre*, for its paradigm, for its
identity. Periodically, it goes through its "identity crisis"
and rediscovers itself. Nowhere else does public administration
go through such soul-searching or experience such self-doubts.

Finally, nowhere else is public administration so misunder-
stood. The environment of public administration is decidedly
unfriendly to it. Traditional American values exhort all that
public administration is not and cannot be. In a country which
once believed that "least government is best government," government management represents, rightly or wrongly, Big Government, bureaucracy, restrictions, taxation, dependency, authority, interference, parasitism, waste, spoils. Admittedly American bureaucracy has its shortcomings and failings, but no matter how well it performs—and to its credit it performs in the
main most admirably—it never performs well enough. In mass
media, it is rarely given the benefit of the doubt. Its motives
are suspect; its actions are detrimental; its results are poor.
It is almost axiomatic that business is better, that private
enterprise is superior, that private organizations are more
economic, efficient, and effective, and that the public sector
is none of these things. No matter how satisfied and uncom-
plaining its clients, public administration cannot shake off
its adverse images and stereotypes. It has to spend, perhaps
justifiably, much effort not only proving that it does and
should exist, but that its performance is good and constantly
improving.

BOUNDARIES OF THE FIELD

These ten factors also affect what public administrators believe should be included within the scope of the field. Opinions, as can be expected, differ widely between minimalists and maximalists. The minimalists want to confine public administration to Wilson's original 1887 conceptualization of a science of (public) administration limited to discovering and applying general principles of good management. Public administration to them is the efficient management of organizations and its objective is improved management of the bureaucracy. In contrast, the maximalists want to expand public administration to its anthropological role of embracing all ways in which society organizes itself to achieve common or collective or public objectives. To them it goes beyond the bureaucracy, beyond the public sector, beyond even the administrative state to include all organizations that carry out public purposes, all policies that are implemented through social organization, and all public affairs, i.e., everything that is subject to collective decisionmaking. It would, in effect, include all social sciences, significant portions of the physical sciences, and some measure of the humanities and arts. The minimalists would confine public administration to public management, only part of administrative science and organization theory, while maximalists would expand it to cover much of the universe of knowledge.

Between these two extremes a center point can be identified where the mainstream of public administration now stands, which is the position that public administration is the formulation and implementation of policies through the public bureaucracy. It no longer confines itself to the execution of policy or the management of bureaucratic systems, but it is reluctant to include the whole science of public policymaking and alternatives to bureaucratic systems of public service delivery. It is not comfortable leaving the solid ground of *process* to embrace *objectives* nor is it willing to go beyond current definitions of the public sector to include third sector organizations, mixed enterprises, and voluntary public services. Its interpretation is wider than government administration but falls well short of all social organization. Its conceptualization covers all activities directly performed by nonpolitical public office holders but not activities performed by members of society, whether or not officials, in a public capacity.

Between minimalists and the centralists (or mainstream American public administration) are those who cannot accept the logic of the administrative state and would like to return public administration to the role of neutral referee or objective regulator. Between the centralists and the maximalists are those propelled by the logic of the administrative state

to go beyond traditional or orthodox public administration to
make the administrative state a more effective instrument of
social engineering. The so-called New Public Administration
Movement of the late 1960's advanced to this position but,
being good democrats all, soon retreated when they realized
their own authoritarian implications. If they could use public
administration to reconstruct American society according to
their egalitarian, participative values, then others could
similarly use it to reconstruct society according to a complete-
ly different set of values, which they would abhor. Nonetheless since their retreat, others looking to enlarge the public
sector and enforce their conception of the public interest over
others' private interests, have replaced them. These would
include within public administration everything that could not
be identified as strictly private without going as far as the
maximalists, whereas their counterparts on the other side of
center would exclude everything that could not be identified
as strictly governmental without going as far as the minimalists.

Along this continuum, there are many other intermediary
points that could be identified according to political beliefs,
economic disposition, social values, religious doctrine, and
culture. Broadly speaking, the ideological Left would tend to
favor the maximalists while the ideological Right would favor
the minimalists, but this would not be true of anti-statist
Marxists who theoretically should favor the minimalists and
pro-statist Fascists who theoretically should favor the maximalists. Strict disciplinarians and paradigm seekers should
veer toward the minimalist position while the inter-discipli-
narians and supra-disciplinarians should lean toward the maxi-
malist position. The current literature takes a predominantly
centrist position, but there are forays on both sides, some
preferring a predominantly public management approach and others
preferring a predominantly administrative state/social engineering approach.

This bibliography of American public administration caters
very much to the center. Minimalists will claim, rightly from
their view, that it covers too much and goes well beyond what
they consider should be in a bibliography of American public
administration. Correspondingly, maximalists will claim, again
rightly from their perspective, that it is too restrictive and
excludes many references that they would expect to find in such
an effort. This bibliography is not addressed to either of them
and it does not meet their requirements. Instead, it endeavors
to portray where public administration is now, in the early
1980's, and where according to the mainstream it would appear
to be going over the next decade. One hopes events will not
soon outdate it, as a similar bibliography constructed a decade
ago would have been.

THE FUTURE OF PUBLIC ADMINISTRATION

Where is public administration heading? What will be its scope a decade hence? In all likelihood, the process of increased government intervention will continue in the United States, but this is not necessarily so. There has been a significant reaction against government irrespective of justification. This reaction in defense of self, private concerns, individual freedom, has been worldwide. Government intervention has run into difficulties. There are clear limitations on what government, any government, can do, and more and more dysfunctions and bureaupathologies of the administrative state are becoming apparent. Governments, public leaders, politicians realize that they have promised too much. They cannot deliver. Worse still, they do not know how to deliver. The price is far higher than they imagined even when they can deliver. In brief, public expectations now outstrip the ability of the administrative state to satisfy them.

In the wake of this, optimism has given way to pessimism. Across the world, there have been attacks on big bureaucracy and taxation. The public is dissatisfied with government; it demands to know what public administration is for and who serves whom. Politicians are dissatisfied with bureaucracy because it lets them down too often. Public managers are unhappy because they see all the internal problems. And the academics who study the field are also dissatisfied. They see the growing gap between the state of the art and practice. All around there is a loss of confidence, a loss of credibility in public institutions, accompanied by demoralization and disillusion. The very legitimacy of public administration is being put to the test.

The current debate is not so much over the management, the administrative side of public administration. That is technological--a science being made out of an art form. It is competent and is seen as growing more competent. Public administration leads in the application of computers and other electronic aids in work processes and decisionmaking. Administrative scientists are finding out how to design better organizations and more effective management systems. Applied behavioral scientists are helping public administrators to change public behavior. Never before have there been so many ideas how to improve the productivity and performance of public organizations. Never before have there been so many administrative reforms awaiting action. The quality of public employees improves as selection procedures become more scientific, public service education and training expands, and merit systems are refined. In all managerial spheres, planning is more effective. Things seem to be in better shape on this side of the ledger.

It is on the public side, the governmental side of public

administration where there is dissention, particularly over the
fundamental question whether modern society is governable any
more and whether the administrative state is out of control.
People point to failures of responsibility and accountability
in public organizations. They discern the need for more effective controls--judicial, legislative, political, financial,
legal, managerial--without handicapping public initiative, enterprise, innovation, and action. They call for more centralization, more decentralization, more bureaucratization, more participation. They want to change the locus of policymaking and
budgeting. At the same time, they desire a more sensitive, aware
and responsive bureaucracy. They do not know whether to place
more faith in national authorities or local authorities and they
are stumped by the large and increasing numbers of semi-autono-
mous, quasigovernment authorities that exist supposedly to solve
particular problems.

People are puzzled by the public side of modern civilization and the role of the public sector in it. They do not
comprehend (and nobody has really bothered to explain it to
them in terms they can understand) the change that has been
and is taking place in the nature of problem solving in contemporary society away from the fire fighter approach to a more
proactive, rather than reactive, stance that requires a new
public administration. To continue further with the old public
administration would severely curb the processes of freedom,
dialectic, and non-violence. But more fundamental is the
question of which problems to leave to public initiative and
which to private initiative. And of those assigned to public
initiative, what alternatives to the administrative state can
be devised? As to the administrative state itself, how can
the public bureaucracy be made more human and humane? How can
contacts between state and citizen be made more fair, just,
speedy, and economical? Can public administration be less
authoritative and more encouraging? How can we get better
public leadership and higher quality policymaking?

The key to the future scope of public administration depends on what answers can be found to these searching basic
questions. Because public administration has assumed that it
knew all the answers or rather that its answers were best or
better, it set itself up for an adversarial relation with its
clients, the public it is supposed to serve. It imposed itself.
It pushed its version of the Good Society, of the public interest, of the common good, and when its clients disagreed, it
treated them like ungrateful, truculent children. Probably
today it knows a little better for it is being punished,
perhaps unjustly, for past sins of arrogance. It needs to
accentuate its positive side more and to overhaul its public
relations. In particular, it has to review carefully and im-

prove the ethics of public office. It has to refurbish its notions of order, equity, and justice. It has to be more forward looking, more creative, more experimental, more entrepreneurial. It has to demonstrate its enhanced capability to manage, to deal with turbulence, and to confront technological risks. Above all, it has to enhance professional responsibility and professional development.

These issues, together with the pressing need to protect public administration against being used as a scapegoat for all social evils, political dilemmas, economic ills, and bad public policies, suggest that the scope of the study of public administration as reflected in the current literature represented in the following chapters, has been drawn too narrowly. There is a general failure to deal with the imperatives of the administrative state, to update the role of the public sector in the mixed economy, to reaffirm the validity of the conception of the common weal as against private interests that still seek to cultivate the public domain as their personal preserve, to demonstrate the effectiveness of public organizations, and to view public administration from the standpoint of the public, not just the administrators. But hope is in sight. The more recent literature does evidence greater awareness of these larger issues. A bolder conception is emerging as rightly befits current practice.

2.
abstracts, indexes, and continuing bibliographies in public affairs and administration

2. ABSTRACTS, INDEXES, AND CONTINUING BIBLIOGRAPHIES IN PUBLIC AFFAIRS AND ADMINISTRATION

Lynn F. Sipe

Public administration lacks a "comprehensive" or unifying medium of bibliographic control comparable to those available for certain other social and natural sciences. This is not altogether surprising considering the continuing "identity crisis" in the discipline discussed in the first chapter, with its varied attempts to reach a consensus as to what it is all about. The situation also suggests the nearly impossible task of bringing bibliographic unity to a discipline that has roots and interests in so many cognate fields of inquiry. The practical implication of this is that the researcher must, of necessity, consult an interdisciplinary range of bibliographic tools to be assured of systematic coverage. In reality, however, those who might most usefully avail themselves of the existing possibilities are frequently unaware of many, if not most, of them.

This chapter is intended as a further step in the direction of bibliographic self-sufficiency for those potential users, particularly for students, faculty, and researchers. That it is not the first step is witnessed by the existence of a number of literature/research guides for the social and political sciences[1] and, in recent years, the appearance of specialized research guides for public administration.[2] The chapter differs from these other contributions in focusing, at greater length and with a more deliberate interdisciplinary emphasis, only on the abstracts, indexes, and continuing bibliographies that can be of value in public administration research.

Titles selected for inclusion offer potential benefit in furthering inquiry in public administration. Public administration is defined as the formulation, implementation, evaluation, and modification of public policy, in both theory and practice, both generally and in its administrative specializations. Consideration is given predominantly to the practice and the teaching of public administration in the United States.

The publications reviewed are of widely varying levels of quality, breadth, and accomplishment.

The number of sources included reflects several considerations. Since public administration is so interdisciplinary in focus, it is essential that bibliographic finding tools from other disciplines should be examined. Among these are publications from the political and social sciences, urban studies, business management, and law. Specialized access tools for government publications, newspapers, and book reviews are also included. Particular attention is given to sources relevant to major administrative specializations in American public administration: health care administration, justice and law enforcement administration, personnel administration, and public finance administration.[3] No matter the excellence of a single tool, no source is all-inclusive and the necessity of consulting multiple sources must be accepted. The existence of similar sources should be acknowledged, if only for variations in format and currency. An important consideration is that the most obvious bibliographic choices for any single inquiry will not always be available locally though alternative choices might be.

Only titles currently published and of a continuing nature are noted, with certain clearly indicated exceptions. Separately published single bibliographies are not considered here. Also excluded from consideration are "national" periodical indexes (e.g., *Canadian Periodical Index*) as well as foreign newspaper indexes and foreign national bibliographies. Each listing provides an essential amount of information about each publication: title (including changes, if any); publisher and place of publication; beginning dates of publication; and a brief narrative description, based on an examination of the most recent issues. Narrative text appearing in quotations is taken from a publication's self-description.

A number of the titles listed can also be searched by computer, through an online bibliographic search service. This service is provided by many libraries and other information agencies, provided they subscribe to the data base offerings of one or more of the major vendors of online search services. In most instances, the individual user will be charged a fee for a computerized literature search, based on a mix of factors: computer and telecommunication connect charges, individual data base charges per citation, and institutional service fees, if any. The advantage of computer searching is vastly increased speed in information retrieval, combined with enhanced precision and greater flexibility in subject searching.

Initials of the three major American online vendors are employed in the online notations, with each listing, to designate which data bases are available from which vendor: LIS = Lockheed Information System (Dialog); SDC = System Development

Corporation (ORBIT); BRS = Bibliographic Retrieval Services. It should be noted that all facilities offering computer-assisted bibliographic searching may not necessarily subscribe to all services. Many of the sources in this chapter are not available online at this time, but may become available for computer searching in the future.[4] Certain highly relevant data bases such as the SCORPIO system at the Library of Congress or other in-house systems in certain government agencies, are considered to be not available as these are not normally accessible from outside of the agency.

The 103 bibliographic sources discussed in this chapter are grouped into thirteen sections, based either on the type of publication or the subjects of the publication they index or list. This arrangement has been selected for the sake of convenience so that like types of indexes or abstracts might be grouped together. Within each section, items are generally listed in order of greatest comprehensiveness or inclusiveness of their listings, reflecting their likely utility to the researcher. Boundaries between the subject/format groups are necessarily judgmental, but not automatically arbitrary. In practice, listings from any one section might well be useful for inquiries focused in other sections.

The chapter, starting with the most general references and moving to more specialized items, is subdivided as follows:

General Sources (Items 1-10);
Newspaper Sources (Items 11-17);
Book Review Sources (Items 18-23);
Social Science Sources (Items 24-33);
Political Science Sources (Items 34-40);
American Government Publications Sources (Items 41-52);
American Public Administration and Management Sources (Items 53-60);
Business Management Sources (Items 61-64);
Justice/Legal/Law Enforcement Administration Sources (Items 65-75);
Public Finance Sources (Items 76-82);
Public Personnel Administration Sources (Items 83-87);
Social Services/Health Care Administration Sources (Items 88-98); and
Urban Administration Sources (Items 99-103).

An alphabetically arranged title index to the contents of this chapter is provided at the end of the volume.

NOTES

1. See especially: Peter Lewis, *The Literature of the Social Sciences* (The Library Association, 1960); Richard Merritt & Gloria Pyszka, *The Student Political Scientist's Handbook* (Cambridge, MA; Schenkman, 1969); Clifton Brook, *The Literature of Political Science* (New York: Bowker, 1969); Robert Harmon, *Political Science: A Bibliographical Guide to Literature* (Metuchen, NJ: Scarecrow Press, 1965-1972); Tze-chung Li, *Social Science Reference Sources* (Westport, CT: Greenwood Press, 1980); and Frederick Holler, *Information Sources of Political Science*, 3rd ed. (Santa Barbara, CA: ABC-Clio Press, 1981).

2. Anthony Simpson, *Guide to Library Research in Public Administration* (New York: Center for Productive Management, John Jay College of Criminal Justice, 1976); Mary G. Rock, *A Handbook of Information Sources and Research Strategies in Public Administration* (San Diego, CA: Institute of Public and Urban Affairs, San Diego State University, 1979); D. A. Cutchin, *Guide to Public Administration* (Itasca, IL: F. E. Peacock Publishers, 1981).

3. Other administrative specializations, such as environmental, public works, transportation, recreation administration, have not been included in this compilation.

4. To keep current with which bibliographic data bases are available online, consult the latest edition of Martha E. Williams et al., eds., *Computer-Readable Databases: A Directory and Sourcebook* (White Plains, NY: Knowledge Industry Publications, 1982). Updated regularly.

GENERAL SOURCES

Listed here are indexes and abstracts that are multi-disciplinary in their subject coverage. Included are indexes to dissertations and to statistics.

1. *Library of Congress Catalog, Books: Subjects.* Publisher/ place varies. 1950-

Each volume in this massive set reproduces Library of Congress printed catalog cards. Arrangement is by subject headings, as assigned by the Library. In numerous instances, Library of Congress subject headings are not as precise or

appropriate to public administration as the researcher might
like, though this is a minor liability. A search here is made
using the same subject headings found in most library card
catalogs. In its totality, this catalog offers the most comprehensive set of listings for monographic works on public
administration topics, based on the collections in American
libraries. Issued quarterly, with annual cumulations. The
annuals are eventually superseded by five-year cumulations.
ONLINE: No

2. *Internationale Bibliographie der Zeitschriften-literatur
   aus allen Gebieten des Wissen*. Osnabrück, West Germany:
   Felix Dietrich Verlag. 1963/64–

   The English language title clearly indicates the range of
this publication's coverage: International Bibliography of
Periodical Literature Covering All Fields of Knowledge. While
German language publications are emphasized, a surprising
number of English and other non-German citations are included.
The classified subject index, "Index Rerum," is arranged by
German language subject headings, with cross-references from
the English term to the appropriate German name. In certain
subject categories a majority of the citations are in English.
At least twelve major subject headings for public administration topics are used in the subject index. There is also a
systematic index of key words, "Index Systematicus," in German,
French, and English. An author index, "Index Autorum" is also
provided. Reference to journal titles in the indexes is by
key numbers. Publication of the multiple volume editions is
twice yearly.
ONLINE: No

3. *Reader's Guide to Periodical Literature*. Bronx, NY:
   H. W. Wilson Co. 1900–

   This is perhaps the one periodical index with which most
library users are familiar, yet it is normally of the least
value to the serious researcher. It emphasizes "selected general interest periodicals" in its coverage, excluding the great
majority of scholarly academic journals. Subjects and authors
are interfiled in a single alphabet. Book reviews are listed
separately at the back of each issue. Issued semi-monthly,
except monthly in February, July, and August, with a bound
annual cumulation each year.
ONLINE: No

4. *Magazine Index*. Menlo Park, CA: Information Access Corp.
   1977–

   Another general interest index to "the periodical titles

most people read." The periodicals covered are approximately
the same as those indexed in *Reader's Guide* (Item 3). Subject
headings and authors are arranged in a single alphabet. More
recent articles are listed first under each heading. Issued
only in a COM (computer output microfilm) format. Each monthly issue represents a cumulation of the entire backfile. The
online version of this index is updated daily in the same
publisher's NEWSEARCH data file.
ONLINE: LIS

   5. *Access: the Supplementary Index to Periodicals.* Evanston,
      IL: John Gordon Burke Publisher, Inc. 1976- Former
      title: *Access: the Index to Little Magazines*, 1976-1978.

      Indexes of this type are useful due to the fact that not
all periodical titles of merit are indexed in the more standard
tools. This publication is "designed to complement the existing general periodical indexes. Its purpose is to provide
information about the contents of magazines not prominently
indexed and held in library collections." Highly specific
subject headings are utilized. A separate author section contains the full bibliographic information for each entry.
Issued three times yearly, with the last issue being the annual
cumulation.
ONLINE: No

   6. *Alternative Press Index.* Baltimore, MD: Alternative Press
      Center, Inc. 1969-

      This "index to alternative and radical publications" pro-
vides access to writings on public issues from a perspective
that is not always considered and that would otherwise be
difficult to document. Primary arrangement of each quarterly
issue is by very specific subject heading. There is no author
index and there are no cumulations. Book reviews are indexed
under a separate heading. An approximate three-year time lag
in publication is a serious liability with this index.
ONLINE: No

   7. *Current Bibliographical Information.* New York: United
      Nations, Dag Hammarskjold Library. 1971-

      Public administration topics are considered by certain
organs of the United Nations. This subject listing from the
U.N. Library includes in its listings sub-sections on "public
administration and management" as well as finance and manpower. Some citations include minimal annotations. Issued
semi-monthly; monthly in July and August. No cumulations. A

good source for researching comparative topics.
ONLINE: No

  8. *Statistical Reference Index*. Washington, DC: Congres-
      sional Information Service, Inc. 1980–

      The frequently awesome task of knowing where to look to
obtain statistics on a particular subject is greatly alleviated
by this index, descriptively subtitled "a selective guide to
American statistical publications from sources other than the
U.S. government." It admirably complements the same publisher's
American Statistics Index (Item 43). All issues appear in two
parts: abstracts and index. The abstracts are arranged according to type of source: associations, business organizations,
commercial publishers, independent research organizations, state
governments, and universities. All forms of publications from
these sources are selectively indexed and abstracted. The indexes are in four parts: "Index by Subjects and Names," indexes
by title and issuing source and an "Index by Categories." This
last index provides subject access by eight types of "geographic breakdowns," six "economic breakdowns" and six "demo-
graphic breakdowns." All indexes cumulate each month during
the quarter. Annual cumulations are also issued.
ONLINE: No

  9. *Dissertation Abstracts International*. Ann Arbor, MI:
      Dissertation Abstracts International. 1938– Former
      titles: *Microfilm Abstracts*, 1938–1951; *Dissertation
      Abstracts*, 1952–1968.

      This essential publication provides "abstracts of disserta-
tions available on microfilm or as xerographic reproductions."
Each issue is in three series: Series A: The Humanities and the
Social Sciences; Series B: The Sciences and Engineering; and
Series C: European Abstracts. Series A and B are based on sub-
missions to the publisher from more than 430 cooperating institutions in North America. Each is arranged by major subject
sections. Public administration dissertations are listed as a
sub-field of political science in Series A. Series C is a
recent innovation (1977). Issued monthly, except for Series
C, which appears quarterly. All have keyword and author indexes. Since 1973 only a cumulated author index has been provided.
ONLINE: BRS, LIS, SDC

  10. *Comprehensive Dissertation Index*. Ann Arbor, MI:
       University Microfilms International. 1973–

      This index differs from *Dissertations Abstracts* in not pro-

viding abstracts and in offering coverage back to 1861. Entries
are grouped by discipline in separate volumes, and then sub-
arranged by keyword subjects within each volume. Public administration is normally subsumed as part of the "Law and Political
Science" listings. A basic set of 37 volumes, covering the
years 1861-1972, was published in 1973. Subsequent annual
supplements have been published since. A nineteen-volume
"1973-1977 Five-Year Cumulation" of the annuals has also been
published. Separate author index volumes appear with all com-
ponents of the set. It is important to note that some listings
do appear in this index that are not included in *Dissertation
Abstracts*.
ONLINE: BRS, LIS, SDC

NEWSPAPER SOURCES

Newspapers contain a wealth of factual analysis and criticism regarding public issues in addition to the "news." With
the indexes cited below, this material becomes easily accessible.

11. *New York Times Index*. New York: New York Times Company.
     1851-

The quality of newspaper indexes varies considerably. Fortunately, as befits the most important American newspaper, this
one is a high-quality product. The index is based on the final
Late City editions of the *Times*, which is also the edition that
is available on microfilm. All entries are filed alphabetically
under the appropriate subject headings, with ample cross-references provided. Entries include brief abstracts for all
news and editorial matter. Reference is made to date of the
issue, page, and column number, with indicators also as to
length of news articles. Issued semi-monthly, with quarterly
and annual cumulations. An unfortunate feature of this, and
most other printed newspaper indexes, is the time lag between
newpaper publication and index publication. In the case of the
Times this can be as long as five months.
ONLINE: See Items 12 and 14

12. *New York Times Information Bank*. Parsippany, NJ: New
     York Times Information Service Inc. 1969-

The New York Times is one of fifty-six publications abstracted in this online information service. Summaries of
major articles from the *Times* are available within 24 hours;
abstracts from the other publications are normally available
within one week of the publication date. Two dozen other newspapers, including major American and foreign titles, are among
the other publications in the data base, as well as major journals of news and opinion. This information service is only

available from the publisher and is not accessible through BRS,
LIS, or SDC.

   13. *Wall Street Journal Index*. New York: Dow Jones.   1958-

      This index is based on the final Eastern edition of the
Journal. Each monthly issue is in two parts: Corporate News
and General News. Each of these is arranged alphabetically
by subject heading. Brief abstracts are included with each
entry. There is an approximate two-month time lag in publication. Annual cumulations are issued.
ONLINE: See Item 94

   14. *National Newspaper Index*. Menlo Park, CA: Information
      Access Corp. 1979-

      The title of this index reflects its indexing coverage
of the three "national" dailies in the United States: *The New
York Times*, *The Christian Science Monitor*, and *The Wall Street
Journal*. Published only in COM (computer output microfilm)
format, each monthly issue of the *Index* cumulates the previous
issues. Arrangement of the entries is by Library of Congress
subject headings. Clear indication is given as to which of
the three newspapers is being cited. Good quality cross-references are provided.
ONLINE: LIS
Note: The online version of this index is updated monthly as
National Newspaper Index and daily, in a separate file called
NEWSEARCH.

   15. *The Official Washington Post Index*. Woodbridge, CT:
      Research Publications, Inc. 1970-

      All name and subject entries are filed in a single
alphabet in this index. One-sentence abstracts are provided
with each entry. Published monthly, with annual cumulations.
ONLINE: SDC
Note: For ONLINE see also Item 12.

   16. *Bell and Howell Index to the [name of newspaper]*.
      Wooster, OH: Bell and Howell, Micro Photo Division.
      Titles/dates vary

      Newspaper Index is a series of indexes to eleven
separate newspapers: *The Christian Science Monitor*,# *Los
Angeles Times*,* *Chicago Sun-Times*, *Denver Post*, *Detroit News*,
Houston Post, *New Orleans Times-Picayune/States Item*, *St. Louis
Post Dispatch*, *San Francisco Chronicle*,* and *The Washington
Post*.* Each separate edition is in two parts: subjects and
personal names. Indication is provided for other than news
stories, noting whether an item is a column, editorial, letter
to the editor, or a review. No form of abstract is provided
with the entries. The quality of the indexing occasionally

leaves something to be desired. Published with a two- to three-
month time lag.
ONLINE: SDC
Note: For ONLINE, #see also Item 14; *see also Item 12.

17. *NewsBank.* Stanford, CT: Newsbank, Inc. 1976-

NewsBank is not a standard newspaper index but "a current
awareness reference service in the field of urban and public
affairs divided into 13 major subject categories." On a monthly basis, articles are selected from over 120 newspapers in
all 50 states, reproduced on microfiche and grouped by subject
matter in printed indexes. The indexes cumulate quarterly and
annually. The index citations refer only to the articles on
microfiche and not to the original source.
ONLINE: Only from publisher

BOOK REVIEW SOURCES

Locating book reviews is a persistent concern, particularly for students. Not all books are reviewed, but the majority
of those that are can be identified through these sources.

18. *Book Review Digest.* Bronx, NY: H. W. Wilson Co. 1905-

The oldest and best-known index to book reviews though
of limited value for public administration book reviews, given
the limited number of political science and public administration journals covered. The *Digest* excerpts reviews from more
than 70 journals. Each issue has a subject and title index.
Issued ten times a year, with quarterly and annual cumulations.
A four-volume author/title index, covering 1905-1974, was published in 1976.
ONLINE: No

19. *Book Review Index.* Detroit: Gale Research Company.
1965-

This source indexes all books reviewed in approximately
330 journals. Valuable for locating public administration
reviews, as several public administration and political science journals are indexed. Arrangement is by the author of
the book reviewed; there is also a title index. Published
bimonthly, with every other issue cumulating the preceding one.
Annual cumulations. A seven-volume "master cumulation" of this
set, covering 1969-1979, was published in 1980-1981. All
citations from the first eleven volumes are included here in
one alphabet.
ONLINE: LIS

20. *Current Book Review Citations.* Bronx, NY: H. W. Wilson Co. 1976-

This is one of the most useful book review indexes, as it emphasizes academic and scholarly titles in its coverage of approximately 1200 journals. Basic arrangement is by author of the book, with a separate title index. No subject or reviewer indexes. Issued 11 times a year with an annual cumulation.
ONLINE: No

21. *Combined Retrospective Index to Book Reviews in Scholarly Journals, 1886-1974.* Arlington, VA: Carrollton Press. 1979-

More than one million book reviews in 459 journals over the period of coverage are cited in this index. Volumes 1-11 index reviews by author of the book. Vols. 12-15 provide a title index. While the number of reviews included here is quite large, the percentage of those reviews devoted to public administration books will be relatively low.
ONLINE: No

22. *Book Review Index to Social Science Periodicals.* Ann Arbor, MI: Perian Press. 1978

This four-volume set is intended to supplement the book review citations appearing in *Social Sciences Index* (Item 25) since 1974, for the period 1964-1973. All reviews are indexed in approximately 280 social science journals. Arrangement is by author of the book; there are no title, subject, or reviewer indexes.
ONLINE: No

23. *Internationale Bibliographie der Rezensionen wissenschaftlicher Literatur.* Osnabrück, West Germany: F. Dietrich Verlag. 1971-

Subtitled "International bibliography of book reviews of scholarly literature," this index complements and is related to the *Internationale Bibliographie der Zeitschriften-Literatur* ... (Item 2). This is the most comprehensive of all the book review indexes, providing coverage of approximately 3000 periodicals in all major areas of scholarly inquiry and in a variety of languages. Certain English language public administration journals are included in this total. Each bi-annual issue is in three volumes. A classified subject index of book reviews, "Index Rerum," includes English and French language cross-references to the appropriate German language subject headings. There are also separate indexes of books reviewed by re-

viewed author and by reviewing author.
Note: In addition to the titles listed above, book review citations are included as a regular feature of various other sources
as noted in this chapter: Items 3, 6, 25, 26, 31, 58, 61, 65,
70, and 73.

SOCIAL SCIENCE SOURCES

    Social science indexes are particularly important to the
researcher, not only because of their coverage of public administration but of cognate disciplines as well.

    24. *Public Affairs Information Service Bulletin.* New York:
         Public Affairs Information Service, Inc. 1915-

        Normally referred to as *P.A.I.S.*, this is the single best
bibliographic access tool to current material in the policy-
oriented social sciences. By its own description, it selectively "indexes periodical articles, books, pamphlets, federal,
state, and local government documents, as well as publications
of public and private agencies, yearbooks and directories, published in English throughout the world." *P.A.I.S.* emphasizes
factual and statistical information in its selection. Issued
twice a month with three quarterly cumulations and an annual
bound volume. Each issue is arranged by subject. Beginning
with the 1977 annual cumulation (volume 63) an annual author
index has been included.
ONLINE: LIS, BRS

    Regarding *P.A.I.S.*, two separately published finding aides
are very useful.

    24A. Wall, C. Edward, comp. and ed. *Public Affairs Informa-*
          tion Service Cumulative Author Index 1965-1969.
          Ann Arbor, MI: Perian Press. 1973

        Similar personal author indexes to the remaining volumes
of the set are contemplated.

    24B. *Cumulative Subject Index to the Public Affairs Informa-*
          tion Service Bulletins 1915-1974. Arlington, VA:
          Carrollton Press. 1977 15 volumes

        This superb cumulation greatly facilitates retrospective
subject searching in the first sixty volumes of *P.A.I.S.* The
volumes are arranged alphabetically. Each subject citation
refers to the year of the annual cumulation in which the complete reference is found, as well as indicating the page and
the item's position on the page.

25. *Social Sciences Index.* Bronx, NY: H. W. Wilson Co.
     1974-

   After *P.A.I.S.* (Item 24), this is the "other" general
social science index. Both author and subject indexing are
provided for "periodicals in the fields of anthropology, area
studies, economics, environmental sciences, geography, law and
criminology, medical sciences, political science, psychology,
public administration, sociology and related subjects." A particularly valuable feature is an author listing of citations to
book reviews included in the journals indexed. Issued four times
a year with an annual bound cumulation.
ONLINE: No

   Social Science Index was preceded by two related titles,
which are important if undertaking retrospective searching.

25A. *International Index.* Bronx, NY: H. W. Wilson Co. 1907-
     March 1965

   Subtitled "A guide to periodical literature in the
social sciences and humanities," this was the first of two indexes antecedent to the current *Social Sciences Index.* Arrangement was similar to the current publication though less detailed
coverage was given to the social sciences and book reviews were
not indexed.

25B. *Social Sciences and Humanities Index.* Bronx, NY:
     H. W. Wilson Co. April 1965-March 1974

   Little variation from the *International Index* in format
or content except for the title change.

26. *Social Sciences Citation Index.* Philadelphia: Institute
     for Scientific Information. 1973-

   This index can be quite confusing to the first-time user
but is worth the patience invested in consulting it. *S.S.C.I.*
is "an international multidisciplinary index to the literature
of the social, behavioral and related sciences." Approximately
4,300 journals are reviewed for indexing as well as selected
significant monographs in the social sciences. Publication is
three times a year with multi-volume annual cumulations. Each
issue is in four parts: Citation Index, Corporate Index, Source
Index, and Permuterm Subject Index. The Citation Index is
arranged by cited author. "The fundamental question one can
answer quickly through the Citation Index is where and by whom
has this paper been cited in the literature." The Corporate
Index lists non-personal cited authors, geographically and by
organizational affiliation. The Source Index is essentially an
index of who did the citing and a list of whom they cited. The
Permuterm Subject Index is a permuted (interchangeable) title-

word index to the works of those authors doing the citing, from
the Source Index.
ONLINE: BRS, LIS, SDC

27. *Current Contents: Social and Behavioral Sciences.*
    Philadelphia: Institute for Scientific Information. 1969–

This is another of the type of index that is based on re-
producing contents pages of journals. Each of its weekly issues
"presents to the reader the titles of papers and all other substantive material from more than 1300 journals reporting world-
wide research and practice in the social and behavioral sciences.'
Each issue is arranged by broad subject categories. A subject
index in each issue "lists in alphabetical order all significant
words from every article title announced in the issue." Author
indexes and address directories are also included. The publication is most useful if consulted regularly as there are no cumulations of any of the indexes.
ONLINE: No

28. *London Bibliography of the Social Sciences.* London:
    Mansell (for British Library of Political and Economic
    Science). 1931–

While not a logical starting point for the average bibliographic inquiry, this can be an excellent back-up resource
for extended social science searches, including many public
administration topics. Arrangement is by a very extensive
variety of subject descriptors. All western languages are included. Books, pamphlets, and documents are listed but NOT
periodical or journal articles. Supplements to the original
basic set of four volumes (1931–32) now appear annually, though
with an approximate two-year time lag.
ONLINE: No

29. *Index to Social Sciences and Humanities Proceedings.*
    Philadelphia: Institute for Scientific Information.
    1979–

Papers presented at the large number of conferences,
seminars, symposia, conventions, etc., held world-wide each year
are published in a variety of media. Prior to the appearance of
this index, there was no easy way to locate much of this material,
particularly in the social sciences. The most significant published proceedings are indexed in this tool. This is a formid-
able work, both in its coverage and in its arrangement. Each
quarterly issue has seven sections. "Contents of Proceedings"
is the main section, arranged by identifying number, with full
descriptive and bibliographic information about each meeting.

A "Category Index" is a very general subject index for scanning
purposes. The "Permuterm Subject Index" is an extremely detailed
"significant word"-type of subject index. Additional indexes
are for author/editor, sponsor, meeting location, and a two-
part corporate name listing. An annual cumulation is published,
with the "Contents of Proceedings" and the "Category Index" in
one volume and the other indexes in the second.
ONLINE: In planning stages

30. *Sociological Abstracts.* San Diego: Sociological Ab-
     stracts, Inc. 1953-

As with other disciplines in the social sciences, the
sociological literature frequently contains studies of interest
to the public administration researcher. This publication is
the leading key to that literature on a world-wide basis. Published five times a year, each issue is arranged hierarchically
in thirty broad subject categories, which are in turn broken
into sub-topics. Among these are "complex organizations (management)," "bureaucratic structures," "delinquency," "planning
and forecasting," "social indicators," and "policy science."
Subject, author, and source indexes are included in each issue.
An annual cumulation of these three indexes is available approximately nine months from the date of the last issue.
ONLINE: LIS

31. *America: History and Life.* Santa Barbara, CA: American
     Bibliographical Center-Clio Press. 1964-

As its title suggests, American history is the primary
focus of this index. Fortunately, that focus is very broadly
defined to include current policy issues so that a number of
public administration interests are encompassed. The publication is issued in four parts each year, at varying intervals.
Part A presents abstracts and bibliographical citations of
articles published world-wide. This Part is arranged schemati-
cally, with separate subject and author indexes. It appears
three times a year. Part B, issued twice yearly, is an index
to book reviews, with separate title and reviewer indexes. Part
C is an annual bibliographic listing, without abstracts, of the
contents of Parts A and B and includes related dissertations.
Part D contains the annual cumulated indexes. Five-year indexes
for 1964-69 and 1969-73 have been published. Some supplementary
issues extend the indexing coverage back in time to 1954.
ONLINE: LIS

32. *Selected Rand Abstracts; a quarterly guide to publica-
     tions of the Rand Corporation.* Santa Monica, CA:
     Rand Corporation. 1963-

The Rand Corporation conducts and publishes a large volume of scientific research and analysis, much of which is directly relevant to the public sector. These abstracts provide
a complete guide to the current unclassified publications from
Rand. These materials are frequently otherwise difficult to
identify. Each issue of the *Abstracts* is divided into a subject
index and a citation section, which includes the abstracts.
Each quarterly issue cumulates the preceding one.
ONLINE: No

Two closely related publications:

32A. *Index of Selected Publications of the Rand Corporation,
     1946-1962* and

32B. *Selected Rand Abstracts, Cumulative Edition, 1963-1972.*

33. *P.A.I.S. Foreign Language Index.* New York: Public Affairs
    Information Service, Inc. 1968-

This foreign language counterpart to the *P.A.I.S. Bulletin*
(Item 24) provides similar coverage for materials published in
French, German, Italian, Spanish, and Portuguese. The first
volume of this publication, covering the years 1968-1971, in-
cludes only articles from periodicals. Published quarterly,
with the fourth issue each year being a cumulated bound volume.
An author index is included in all issues.
ONLINE: LIS, BRS

POLITICAL SCIENCE SOURCES

Public administration is considered a sub-field of political
science by many academicians. Political science indexes are,
therefore, essential to any public administration literature
search.

34. *International Political Science Abstracts.* Paris:
    International Political Science Association. 1951-

A comprehensive abstracting publication, international
and multilingual in coverage, including references only to
journal articles. Abstracts for non-English language articles
are in French. Each bi-monthly issue is arranged by six broad
topical categories. Of these, the "government and administrative institutions" section is the most germane to public administration. A detailed subject index is included in each issue.
This is cumulated annually and added to it is an annual author
index. A particularly valuable tool for comparative studies.
ONLINE: No

35. *ABC POL SCI*. Santa Barbara, CA: American Bibliographic
    Center-Clio Press. 1969-

The abbreviated title stands for Advanced Bibliography
of Contents: Political Science. This index reproduces edited
tables of contents of approximately 300 journals. Most of the
journals covered are in English. Excellent author and subject
indexes in each issue facilitate use of the reproduced tables
of contents, which are themselves arranged alphabetically by
journal title. Issued five times a year plus an annual index.
A five-year index, to volumes 1-5, 1969-1973, has also been
issued.
ONLINE: No

36. *International Bibliography of Political Science*.
    London: Tavistock Publications. 1954-

This is one of four specialized titles in the UNESCO
sponsored International Bibliography of the Social Sciences.
Issued annually, the *Bibliography* is selective but "sufficiently
complete" in its coverage. Publications in most major languages
are listed; an English language title is provided if the original
is not in English. No abstracts are included but one can frequently find cross-references to the abstracts published in the
International Political Science Abstracts (Item 34). Each volume is hierarchically arranged within six broad subject groupings, one of which is entitled "government and public administration." Author and subject indexes (English and French) are provided. The publication usually appears 2-3 years after the
cover date.
ONLINE: No

37. *United States Political Science Documents*. Pittsburgh,
    PA: University of Pittsburgh, University Center for Inter-
    national Studies. 1975-

A selective index to the journal literature in political
science. Its philosophy is that it is better to provide more
in-depth indexing coverage of the most significant part of the
journal literature than to attempt to be inclusive in coverage.
Each annual edition is in two parts. The first includes a "ro-
tated subject descriptor display" and indexes by author, subject,
geographic area, proper corporate name, and journal. Part two
contains the documents, descriptors or abstracts of the documents
cited. Unique to these abstracts are indications of any special
features in the original and a list of cited people. A number
of public administration journals are included in this form of
in-depth indexing.
ONLINE: LIS, SDC

38. *Universal Reference System.* New York: IFI/Plenum Data
    Company. 1966-

    This is the printed output from another computerized
information retrieval service in political science. The system
consists of a basic set of 10 volumes, issued in 1966, with subsequent annual supplements of 2-3 volumes each. Each supplement
contains a list of the subject terms employed in the index, abstracts of all documents (books and periodicals) indexed, and a
bibliographical (subject) index to the abstracts. An author
index is also included. As with other computerized compilations,
more in-depth subject indexing is possible than with conventional
means. This can be an extremely useful tool for researching
certain public administration topics.
ONLINE: No

39. *Bulletin Analytique de Documentation Politique Economique
    et Social Contemporaine.* Paris: Fondation Nationale des
    Sciences Politique. 1946-

    The standard French political science bibliography, most
particularly of value for comparative studies. A selective
and somewhat eclectic publication. Each of the eleven issues
annually is arranged in two classified sections. Articles on
public administration topics will be found sub-arranged by
country in the first of these: "Problemes Nationaux." A subject
index is available only in the final issue of the year and not
in the numbers preceding it.
ONLINE: No

40. *C.R.I.S.: The Combined Retrospective Index to Journals
    in Political Science, 1886-1974.* Washington, DC:
    Carrollton Press. 1977-78

    This eight-volume set is not an on-going publication
but is sufficiently important to merit its inclusion here.
C.R.I.S. is a retrospective index to 531 selected English language journals in political science, history, and sociology.
Volumes 1-6 of the set contain the subject indexing, gathered
in 95 broad categories and sub-arranged by keyword. Of the
six subject volumes, four are devoted to public administration
related topics, very broadly defined. Volumes 7 and 8 contain
the author indexes.
ONLINE: No

AMERICAN GOVERNMENT PUBLICATIONS SOURCES

    Government publications represent an invaluable, but
frequently untapped, resource for public policy research. The

tools listed here greatly facilitate access to this material.

41. *Monthly Catalog of United States Government Publications.*
    Washington, DC: Superintendent of Documents. 1895–
    Title has varied.

This is the basic access tool for many publications of
the United States government, particularly those published by
the Government Printing Office. It is essential to note, however, that this is not a comprehensive listing of all United
States government publications. Basic arrangement of each
monthly issue is by issuing agency or office of the government.
Six separate indexes facilitate access to the contents of each
issue: author, title, subject, series/report, stock number, and
title key word. Such detailed index access has only become
available in recent years of this publication. The indexes are
cumulated semi-annually and annually.
ONLINE: LIS
Note: A number of cumulated or special author or topical access
indexes to the *Monthly Catalog* have been issued by commercial
publishers. Inquiries should be made of a library's Government
Documents Dept.

42. *CIS/Index to Publications of the United States Congress.*
    Washington, DC: Congressional Information Service, Inc.
    1970–

Congressional documents, including hearings, contain a
wealth of information and analysis relevant to almost all aspects
of public policy interest. This outstanding index provides "a
complete information retrieval system to the working papers of
the United States Congress." Published monthly, each issue is
in two parts: the Index Book and the Abstracts Book. The
Index Book contains a variety of indexes to the Congressional
output: "Subjects and Names, " "Titles," "Bill, Report, and
Document Numbers," and an "Index of Committee and Subcommittee
Chairmen." Reference is normally made from the Index Book
to the Abstracts Book, which is arranged by special abstract
code numbers, included with the index listings. Detailed abstracts describe each document listed. Indexes cumulate quarterly and annually. The abstracts are included with the annual
index cumulation in the *CIS/Annual*. Five-year (1970-1974) and
four-year (1975-1978) Cumulative Indexes have also been issued.
ONLINE: LIS, SDC

43. *American Statistics Index.* Washington, DC: Congressional
    Information Service, Inc. 1973–

Prior to the appearance of this publication it was quite
difficult to access the tremendous amount of statistical informa-

tion published by the federal government. The *A.S.I.* has largely solved that problem, providing a "master guide and index" to
statistics appearing in federal publications. Statistics are
indexed from all forms of government printed media, including
periodicals, annual reports, special studies, and Congressional
documents. A base edition for this service, known as the *A.S.I.*
Retrospective Edition, published in 1974, "provides detailed
and comprehensive coverage of federal government statistical
publications currently in print as of January 1, 1974, as well
as of significant publications issued since the early 1960's."
The retrospective set has since been complemented by Monthly
Supplements, which cumulate into Annual Supplements. Both types
of supplements are issued in two parts. The Index provides a
"Subject and Name Index," a "Category Index," a "Title Index,"
and an "Agency Report Number Index." Index references lead to
the Abstracts, which provide excellent descriptions for each
publication indexed. The abstracts are arranged by abstract
number, as provided in the Index.
ONLINE: LIS, SDC

44. *Index to U.S. Government Periodicals*. Chicago:
     Infordata International. 1970–

     A general interest periodical index but one covering
only periodicals produced by more than 100 federal government
agencies. "The interest of the publishers is to provide access
to every one of the U.S. government periodicals which offers
substantive articles of lasting research and reference value."
Approximately 12 percent of federal government periodicals are
thus included in the indexing. Federal agency publications
frequently present unique in-house perspectives on public issues,
and this index simplifies retrieval. Subjects and authors are
filed together in a single alphabet. Published quarterly, with
the final issue being an annual cumulation.
ONLINE: No

45. *Government Reports Announcements & Index*.
     Springfield, VA: National Technical Information Service.
     1946– Title has varied.

     This biweekly publication provides summaries of all
current declassified government-sponsored research. Each issue
is arranged in twenty-two subject categories, which are further
subdivided. Two of the major categories of direct interest here
are Category 5: Behavioral and Social Sciences, and Category 6:
Biological and Medical Sciences (re: health care administration).
Five indexes appear in each issue: subject, personal author,
corporate author, contract number, and NTIS Order/Report Number. These same indexes cumulate as the multi-volume *Govern-*

ment Reports Annual Index. Many of the reports listed here
have not been published elsewhere and are available only from
NTIS.
ONLINE: BRS, LIS, SDC
Note: Regarding online searching of this index, NTIS publishes
annual listings of "Published Searches" from its data base, which
are available for sale. A variety of these deal with subjects
covered in the public administration relevant sections noted
above.

46. *NTIS Abstract Newsletters.* Springfield, VA: National
     Technical Information Services. Dates of issues vary.

     This is not a single title but a series of twenty-six
separate subject listings, presenting summaries of most unclassified federally funded research as it is completed and made
available to the public. The *Newsletters* offer more convenient
subject handling of the NTIS reports than is available in the
title listed above (Item 45), which is comprehensive in its
coverage. The *Newsletters* titles of direct relevance to public
administration include "Administration and Management"; "Behavior
and Society"; "Energy"; "Health and Planning and Health Services Research"; and "Problem-Solving Information for State
and Local Governments." Substantial abstracts are provided with
each listing. Most *Newsletters* are issued weekly, with the
final issue of the year being an annual subject index.
ONLINE: BRS, LIS, SDC

47. *Federal Index.* Cleveland, OH: Predicasts, Inc. 1976-

     While this index covers more than just government pub-
lications, its major focus is on certain key federal titles.
It "covers the basic information sources published by the Federal Government" by indexing major statements, actions, and
rulings. Selective coverage is provided for the *Congressional Record*, the *Federal Register*, and the *Weekly Compilation
of Presidential Documents*. Also included in this coverage is
the *Washington Post* and approximately 87 trade, industry, and
financial publications which "provide analysis and alternative
points of view to the government documents." This type of pre
sentation makes this an extremely useful resource for locating
current information on federal activities and collateral analysis in a single publication. Each monthly issue is arranged
in three sections: "The Federal Government" (the acting federal
agency); "Government Functions" (policy or programs); "Industry
and Society" ("people, groups, industries and institutions
affected"). Cumulated annually.
ONLINE: LIS, SDC

48. *Monthly List of GAO Reports.* Washington, DC: U.S.
     General Accounting Office. 197?-

     The General Accounting Office conducts numerous manage-
ment audits and surveys of federal agencies, programs, practices,
and policies each year. The resulting reports can provide a rich
source of policy and program information. This publication provides abstracts of all GAO reports issued during a given month.
Arrangement is by broad topical groupings. No indexes of cumulations. See also below.
ONLINE: No

49. *General Accounting Office Publications.* Washington,
     DC: U.S. General Accounting Office. 196?-

     This is a semi-annual listing of GAO reports issued in
a six-month period. It differs from the *Monthly List* above
in that no abstracts are provided. Arrangement is by broad
subject categories, with a separate agency index in each issue.
ONLINE: No

50. *Monthly Checklist of State Publications.* Washington,
     DC: Library of Congress, Gifts and Exchange Division.
     1910-

     While most state governments issue their own publications
catalogues, this is a much more practical source for its listing of documents from all fifty states. The *Checklist* is not
a complete record of all state publications but "a record of
state documents issued during the last five years which have
been received by the Library of Congress." Arrangement within
each monthly issue is by state and then by issuing agency of
the state government. No indexes are published with the monthly issues. There are no cumulations but an annual combined
subject/geographic index is issued during the following year.
ONLINE: No
Note: Mention should be made of an additional title which indexes state documents.

50A. *Checklist of State Publications.* Englewood, CO:
     Information Handling Services. 1977- quarterly

51. *State Government Research Checklist.* Lexington, KY:
     Council of State Governments. 1959- Former title:
     Legislative Research Checklist, 1959-1978.

     This modest but very useful publication is not an index
to state publications as such but rather a listing of "research
reports by legislative service agencies and other study committees and commissions in the states." Publications from the

Advisory Commission on Intergovernmental Relations, the Council
of State Governments, and selected studies from university research bureaus are also included. Each bimonthly issue is
arranged by a broad variety of policy and political subject
headings. There are no indexes or cumulations.
ONLINE: No

52. *Index to Current Urban Documents.* Westport, CT:
    Greenwood Press. 1972-

The index "makes available complete and detailed bibliographic descriptions of the majority of the known local
government documents issued annually by the largest cities and
counties in the United States and Canada." State publications
are not normally included. Approximately 272 of the largest
cities and counties are now included in the coverage. Published
quarterly, with the final issue of the volume serving as an
annual cumulation. Arrangement is geographical, by city or
county, followed by a subject index. While this is a very
valuable information source it should be emphasized that it is
not comprehensive in its listing of publications from any juris-
diction.
ONLINE: No

AMERICAN PUBLIC ADMINISTRATION AND MANAGEMENT SOURCES

The brevity of this listing of bibliographic finding
tools specific to public administration emphasizes the necessity to consult indexes "outside" the discipline in any serious
research.

53. *Sage Public Administration Abstracts.* Beverly Hills,
    CA: Sage Publications, Inc. 1974-

A quarterly journal of abstracts of "important recent
literature" in the field of public administration. Each issue
contains approximately 250 abstracts, selected from over 170
journals which the publisher regularly scans. Certain books,
pamphlets, government publications, significant speeches, and
legislative research studies are also covered. Each issue
contains subject and author indexes, which are cumulated in
the last number of each volume. Its limited coverage and frequently non-specific subject indexing compromise the value of
an otherwise useful source.
ONLINE: No

54. *Recent Publications on Governmental Problems.* Chicago:
    Charles E. Merriam Center for Public Administration
    Library. 1932-

A very useful semi-monthly listing of recent "books, periodical articles, pamphlets, federal, state and local documents, and publications of public and private agencies as well as commercial and trade sources" on "governmental problems," broadly defined. Each issue is arranged in nine broad subject categories: reference, energy and environment, finance and taxation, housing and building, law enforcement and criminal justice, personnel, planning, public works and utilities, and general public administration. Commencing in 1978 (volume 47) annual cumulations, with subject, author, and title indexes, have been issued. Many of the 900 periodicals selectively indexed in *R.P.G.P.* are not indexed in other indexes.
ONLINE: No

55. *Bibliographie Internationale de Science Administrative/ International Bibliography of Administrative Science.* Paris: Centre Nationale de la Recherche Scientifique, Centre de Documentation Sciences Humaines. 1941– Former title: *Bulletin Signaletique: Science Administrative,* vols. 1–31, 1941–1977.

An outstanding bibliographic product, both in terms of its comprehensiveness and its organization. Most citations refer to journal articles, with some monographs included. International in its coverage, all titles are listed in the original language as well as French. All of the abstracts are in French only. Each quarterly issue is arranged or sub-arranged within seven broad categories: administrative science, history, methods of administrative science, administrative structures, civil service, means of administrative actions, and control of public administration. Subject and author indexes are provided quarterly and annually; since 1978 (volume 32) these are published in separate English and French versions.
ONLINE: Not in the United States

56. *From the ACIR Library: Periodical Index.* Washington, DC: U.S. Advisory Commission on Intergovernmental Relations Library. 196?–

This monthly periodical index, of quite modest coverage, is occasionally useful. Its subject focus is not confined to intergovernmental relations, but rather to the broad range of public policy issues of interest to the Advisory Commission. Entries are arranged under upwards of forty subject headings. Unfortunately, no abstracts are provided and there are no cumulations.
ONLINE: No

57. *The Municipal Yearbook*, "Sources of Information" chapter. Chicago: International City Management Association. 1975-

     Though published since 1934, it was only in 1975 that the *Yearbook* added this significant annual feature. A "selected bibliography for major areas of local government administration ... these listings are compiled for reference primarily for urban administrators, staff members of governmental research bureaus and other research and service organizations, and staff members of state and federal agencies with a direct involvement in urban affairs." The entries are arranged in 16 subject categories. While not all subject interests of public administration are covered in these special chapters, this can be a very useful source, particularly for practitioners in the field. The "Sources of Information" chapters in the 1975 and 1976 volumes retrospectively extend the bibliographic coverage back to 1970.
ONLINE: No

58. *Documentation in Public Administration*. New Delhi: Indian Institute of Public Administration. 1973-
    Supersedes: *Public Administration Abstracts and Index of Articles*.

     A broad spectrum of journal articles from the major English speaking countries are indexed in this quarterly publication. Abstracts of varying length are provided for 40-50 percent of the articles listed. Arrangement is by a variety of highly specific subject headings. Each issue includes an author index for the journal articles. In addition, a separate "Book Notes" section offers brief abstracts of 40-50 books per issue, arranged by author. Finally, there is an index to book reviews; the vast majority of the reviews are from journals published in India. Even with its Indian bias this is a good back-up tool as many titles are indexed here that are missed in many of the more standard sources.
ONLINE: No

     Library acquisitions lists can serve as excellent subject bibliographies if the library collects comprehensively in its subject areas. Two leading examples of this type of publication are noted below; certain others appear in this chapter in the other subject sections.

59. *Accessions List of the Library of the Institute of Government Studies*. Berkeley, CA: University of California, Institute of Governmental Studies Library. Date ?-

An acquisitions listing from the finest American library
of its type. The Institute's list is particularly valuable because of the Library's policy of primarily collecting pamphlets,
research reports, and special studies from or pertaining to all
levels of government throughout the United States. Each monthly
list is arranged by subject; there are no cumulations or indexes.
ONLINE: No

For the period prior to 1971, the Library's Subject Catalog
has been published by the G. K. Hall Company (Boston), presenting an historical, cumulated record of holdings for the years
1918-1970. The Subject Catalog is arranged by subject and includes indexing of the Library's substantial periodical holdings.
A "First Supplement" to the I.G.S. Catalog was published in 1978,
in five volumes, covering the years 1970-1977.

60. Royal Institute of Public Administration. *Library
     Accessions List*. London, 1971?-

Issued quarterly by the leading British library in
public administration, this list provides a good overview of
recently published books and articles in public administration.
While a British bias is to be expected, a large number of
American publications are covered. Arrangement is by 25-30
broad subject headings, organized systematically and not alphabetically. No cumulations of indexes.
ONLINE: No

BUSINESS MANAGEMENT SOURCES

Management in the private sector has always contributed
richly to theory and practice in public administration. Access
to this literature is through the following sources.

61. *Business Periodicals Index*. Bronx, NY: H. W. Wilson Co.
     1958-

"Management and personnel administration" are among the
public administration interests covered in this basic index to
the journal literature in the field of business. Approximately
265 English language journals are indexed here on a regular
basis. The main body of the index is arranged by subject entry,
with a separate author listing for citations to book reviews.
Published eleven times a year, with quarterly and annual cumulations.
ONLINE: No

62. *The Business Index.* Menlo Park, CA: Information Access
    Corporation. 1980-

    This is the most comprehensive index to the business
literature. It is not published in traditional paper format
but instead is issued in a COM (computer output microfilm)
edition, read on a special viewer, which is supplied with the
subscription. Its coverage includes books, some government
documents, complete indexing of over 500 business periodicals
and selected indexing of an additional 1000 general interest
and legal periodicals. Certain financial newspapers are also
indexed. Abstracts are provided for those publications indexed
in *Management Contents* (Item 63). Indexing coverage extends
back to January 1979. Subjects, names, and times are arranged
in a single alphabet. Abstracts, as available, are in "register" number order. Each monthly microfilm issue totally cumulates and updates the preceding issue.
ONLINE: No

63. *Management Contents.* Skokie, IL: Management Contents,
    Inc. 1975-

    Each issue of this publication "contains the table of
contents of the latest issues of the finest business/management
periodicals available.... It is intended to fill the need for
an economic approach to the most current information ... to
aid decision-making and forecasting." Public administration
is one of the broad subject areas included. It is published
every other week. Arrangement is by journal title, with a
subject index provided. An annual index is also issued.
ONLINE: BRS, SDS, LIS

64. *ABI/INFORM.* Louisville, KY: Data Courier, Inc. August
    1971-

    This data base is not available in published form and
is only available online. "General decision sciences" information is stressed in its indexing coverage of approximately
400 periodicals in business management and administration.
Abstracts are provided with each citation. This is perhaps a
more useful source to consult, if searching online, than the
similar online version of *Management Contents* (Item 63).
ONLINE: LIS

JUSTICE/LEGAL/LAW ENFORCEMENT ADMINISTRATION SOURCES

    Law journals represent a frequently neglected resource
in bibliographic research, yet the legal literature is rich with
writings on a broad range of public and administrative issues.

Justice and law enforcement administrators can depend on both
their own specialized indexes and relevant portions of the
criminology and police indexes for bibliographic coverage.

65. *Criminal Justice Periodical Index.* Ann Arbor, MI:
    University Microfilms International. 1975–

An excellent index, emphasizing North American periodicals specific to the criminal justice field. It provides particularly good coverage of newsletters and reporting services
in addition to the professional and academic journals. Full
bibliographic citations are provided in both the author and
subject indexes. The subject index is notable for its highly
specific subject headings. Reviews are indexed under the subject headings "book reviews," "film reviews" and "periodical
reviews." Published three times a year, with the final issue
being the annual cumulation.
ONLINE: LIS

66. *Criminal Justice Abstracts.* Hackensack, NJ: National
    Council on Crime and Delinquency. 1968– Former title:
    Crime and Delinquency Literature, 1968–1976.

Each issue of this publication "contains in-depth abstracts of current literature, worldwide in scope, and a comprehensive [literature] review that synthesizes and summarizes the
knowledge on or developments in a certain subject." This is a
highly selective index, with only 150–160 publications covered
in a typical issue, including monographs, research reports, and
journal articles. For those items included, unusually lengthy
abstracts of up to a page are provided. Arrangement is by one
of six broad topical groupings. The *Abstracts* appear quarterly,
with a subject index in each issue and a cumulative subject index for the year in the final issue. There are no author indexes.
ONLINE: No

67. *Criminology and Penology Abstracts.* Amstelveen, Nether-
    lands: Kugler Publications. 1961– Former titles:
    Excerpta Criminologica, 1961–1968; *Abstracts on Crim-
    inology and Penology,* 1969–1979.

A comprehensive tool, citing both books and articles.
This is the international abstracting service "covering the
etiology of crime and juvenile delinquency, the control and
treatment of offenders, criminal procedure and the administration of justice." Abstracts of varying length are provided
for most but not all of the citations. All abstracts are in
English even when the original is not. Each bi-monthly issue
is arranged under 13 broad topical headings, with excellent

subject and author indexes. Cumulated indexes are included in issue number six each year.
ONLINE: No

68. *Current Law Index.* Menlo Park, CA: Information Access Corp. 1980-

This is a printed index covering the same extensive group of law journals included in the same publisher's *Legal Resource Index* (Item 73). The actual indexing and arrangement are identical in both sources, with this index excluding material from the general and academic journals, legal and other newspapers, monographs and government documents. Published monthly, with quarterly and annual cumulations.
ONLINE: LIS

69. *Document Retrieval Index.* Washington, DC: United States Department of Justice, National Criminal Justice Reference Service. 1972-

The *Document Retrieval Index* contains information on all additions to the N.C.J.R.S. collection of published and unpublished literature and audio-visual material in the field of criminal justice. Many of the items listed are published abroad. The *Index* is now issued only in mocrofiche. There are five sections in each issue: "Document Citations"; "Subject Index"; "Personal Name Index"; "Title Index"; and the "NCJ Thesaurus." Abstracts of the documents listed are not provided; see the following item in this regard. A cumulative edition of the *D.R.I.* has been published for the years 1972-1978. Commencing with 1979, annual supplements, in the same format as the cumulation, have been issued.
ONLINE: LIS

70. *Index to Legal Periodicals.* Bronx, NY: H. W. Wilson Co., 1908-

While no longer the preeminent legal periodical index, this is still a valuable source because of its long publishing history. The *Index* provides coverage for over 300 "legal periodicals published in the United States and Canada, Great Britain, Ireland, Australia and New Zealand ... if they regularly publish legal articles of high quality and permanent reference value." Articles from yearbooks and other annuals are also included. Subjects and authors are indexed in a single alphabetical arrangement. Published eleven times a year, with quarterly, annual, and triennial cumulations.
ONLINE: No

71. *Index to Periodical Articles Related to Law*. Dobbs
    Ferry, NY: Glanville Publications. 1959–

    Articles selected for indexing here are not normally in-
dexed in the *Index to Legal Periodicals* (Item 70). "Law" is
broadly defined in reference to the social and behavioral
sciences and thus touches on many public policy issues. Each
quarterly issue has separate subject and author sections. The
final issue of the year is the annual cumulation. Multi-year
cumulations cover 1958–1968, 1969–1973, and 1974–1978.
ONLINE: No

72. *Legal Contents*. Northbrook, IL: Management Contents,
    Inc. 1972– Former title: *Contents of Current Legal
    Periodicals*, 1972–Dec. 1980.

    A bi-weekly current awareness publication which repro-
duces the contents pages of more than 300 major legal periodicals. Arrangement of each issue is by title of the journal,
with a separate subject index to the articles by field of law.
No cumulations.
ONLINE: BRS, LIS, SDC, as part of the Management Contents data
base.

73. *Legal Resource Index*. Menlo Park, CA: Information
    Access Corp. 1980–

    Like *The Business Index* (Item 62), this publication is
issued only in a COM (computer output microfilm) format. It
covers almost twice the amount of core legal literature as the
Index to Legal Periodicals (Item 70). More than 680 English language journals are indexed comprehensively as well as six legal
newspapers. In addition, selective indexing coverage is provided for general periodicals and newspapers, if the articles
are relevant to law. Important legal monographs, government
documents, and articles from academic journals are also selectively covered. Each monthly COM issue totally cumulates and
supersedes the previous one. Issues are arranged in four
sections: subjects, author/title, cases, and statutes. The
subject section comprises over 60 percent of each issue. Book
reviews are indexed in the author/title section.
ONLINE: LIS

74. *Police Science Abstracts*. Amstelveen, Netherlands:
    Kugler Publications. 1973– Former title: *Abstracts
    on Police Science*. 1973–1979.

    This is another international abstracting service "cov-
ering police science, the forensic sciences and forensic medicine." Both books and articles are cited though an abstract

is not provided in all cases. All abstracts are in English
regardless of the language of the original. The issues are
arranged under six broad topical headings; the bulk of the
coverage is devoted to "police organization" and "police operations." High-quality subject and author indexes are provided,
which cumulate in the final number of each volume. Published
bi-monthly.
ONLINE: No

75. *SNI: Selective Notification of Information.* Washington,
     DC: United States Department of Justice, National Crimi-
     nal Justice Reference Service. 1967?-

     SNI "announces the most significant documents and audio-
visual materials added to the data base of the National Criminal Justice Reference Service during the previous month." It
is particularly useful as it emphasizes timely and comprehensive "research reports, program descriptions, standards, pro-
gram/project evaluation criteria, and works that provide solutions to specific criminal justice problems." Each monthly
issue is arranged by 22 major subject areas. All citations
include a lengthy abstract. The monthly issues include no indexes. Cumulations for 1972-1978, and annually thereafter, are
arranged by NCJ number, with subject, author, and title indexes
following.
ONLINE: LIS, as part of the larger N.C.J.R.S. data base.

PUBLIC FINANCE SOURCES

    Public finance has few separate indexing media but is
reasonably well served by a variety of economic indexes and
abstracts.

76. *Journal of Economic Literature.* Nashville, TN:
     American Economic Association. 1963- Former title:
     Journal of Economic Abstracts, 1963-1968.

     Prior to its title change, this was exclusively an
abstracting journal. Now approximately 25 percent of each
quarterly issue is devoted to two or three research articles
and a classified section of lengthy book reviews. The focus
of the bulk of each issue is bibliographic, consisting of a
classified and annotated listing of new books plus a three-
part listing of current periodicals. The periodicals section
lists the contents of current periodicals arranged by journal
title in one section and by classified subject listing in a
second. Abstracts of selected articles, from the subject section and prepared by the original authors, comprise the final

portion of the periodicals list. The abstracts section is
arranged in the same classified order as the subject section.
Included as part of the subject classifications are the following public finance and administration categories: "Fiscal
theory and policy," "Public finance," "Organization and decision theory," "Business and public administration," and "Labor
markets, public policy." An index of all authors in the periodicals section is provided. The annual index lists "authors
of articles, reviews, communications, and abstracts" but not
authors of articles listed but not abstracted. There are no
cumulations of any of the quarterly sections.
ONLINE: LIS

77. *Index of Economic Articles in Journals and Collective*
    Volumes. Homewood, IL: Richard D. Irwin. 1961–
    Former title: *Index of Economic Articles*, 1962-1968.

Sponsored by the American Economic Association, this
title is closely related to the *Journal of Economic Literature*
(*J.E.L.*, Item 76). Most journals indexed here are also indexed
in the *J.E.L.* Articles from collective volumes represent those
abstracted in the *J.E.L.* There are significant differences
between the two publications, however. Only English language
articles are included in the *Index*. The classification system
for subject arrangement is much more detailed and precise in
the *Index* than in the *J.E.L.* "Fiscal Theory and Policy, Public
Finance" is the most specifically relevant here of the 320
classification groupings, though a number of sub-groupings
of other sections are also of interest. Abstracts are not
provided in the *Index*. An author index to the subject listings
is included. This source is much less current than the *J.E.L.*;
the volume for 1976 was published in 1980. Retrospective
volumes of this set extend the indexing coverage back to 1886.
ONLINE: LIS

78. *International Bibliography of Economics.* London:
    Tavistock Publications, 1952–

Like the *International Bibliography of Political Science*
(Item 36), this is one of the four specialized titles in the
UNESCO sponsored International Bibliography of the Social
Science series. As an annual publication, it is selective but
"sufficiently complete" in its coverage. Primary relevance
to public finance comes with the broad topical listings for
"Social economics and policy" and "Public economy." Publications in most major languages are included, making this a particularly valuable tool for comparative finance studies. English translations of titles are provided for books and periodi-

cals not in English. Author and subject indexes, in English
and French, are at the back of each volume. There is normally a 2-3-year time delay in publication from the cover date.
ONLINE: No

79. *Resources in Review.* Washington, DC: Government
Finance Research Center of the Municipal Finance
Officers Association. 1979–

This occasionally useful bibliographic newsletter
provides a sampling of the recent literature on public finance.
It is issued bi-monthly. The "Highlights" section discusses
in some detail the results of various studies, published proceedings, etc. A "Recent Acquisitions" section offers book
reviews of current literature in finance and financial management. The bulk of each issue is an "annotated bibliography"
of separately published monographs and studies, arranged by
very general subject headings. There are no indexes or cumulations.
ONLINE: No

80. *Key to Economic Science and Management Sciences.*
The Hague, Netherlands: Nijhoff. 1953– Former title:
Economic Abstracts, 1953–1975.

Monographs, reports, and journal articles are noted in
this "semi-monthly review (with annual indexes) of abstracts
on economics, finance, trade, industry, foreign aid, management, marketing and labour." Within the index, public finance
is a sub-section of the "Economics" listings. There is also
a separate "Law, Public Administration" section. While this
publication is of variable utility for many public finance
inquiries, the following subject terms beginning with the word
"public" appear in the annual index: administration, debt,
decision-making, enterprises, expenditure, finance, goods,
and investments.
ONLINE: LIS, as part of the Economic Abstracts International
Data Base.

81. *Bibliographie der Wirtschaftwissenschaften.*
Göttingen, West Germany: Vandenhoeck and Ruprecht.
1905–

Since 1968 this monument of German bibliographic endeavor has carried the subtitle "Internationale Dokumentation
der Buch- und Zeitschriften literatur der Wirtschaftswissen-
schaften." It is a classified, worldwide bibliography of
economic literature, quite broadly defined. Primarily covering journal articles, numerous books and government documents

are included as well. As of 1978, the *Bibliographie* appears
in two semi-annual volumes. All tables of contents, section
headings, and indexes (subject/regional and alphabetical or
author-title) are in both German and English. The bibliographic entries are in their original language. Within the subject
classifications are sections covering "Economic policy," "Public finance," and "Social policy, public health, education,
sciences, and technology." Subdivisions within other classifications would also be of interest to public finance or
administration.

82. *Documentation Economique; Revue Bibliographique de
    Synthèse*. Paris: Institut National de la Statistique
    et des Etudes Economiques. 1942-

This French publication can be of some use in accessing
public finance studies that have appeared in the principal
economic reviews, French and foreign. It presents another
classified arrangement, with its Section 5 devoted to "Monnaie
et Finances Publiques." Issued bi-monthly, with the citations
printed on perforated index cards, bound together. There are
author and subject indexes in each issue, but there are no
annual cumulations of any type.
ONLINE: No

PUBLIC PERSONNEL ADMINISTRATION SOURCES

Public personnel administration is bibliographically
a sub-field of the larger topic of personnel administration
and is normally treated as such in the existing personnel and
labor indexes.

83. *Personnel Literature*. Washington, DC: Office of Per-
    sonnel Management, Library, 1941-

Materials received in the library of the United States
Office of Personnel Management, formerly the Civil Service
Commission, are noted in this essential publication. The
monthly issues are arranged topically under at least seventy
different subject headings. Both books and articles are included. There are no indexes with the monthly issues but there
are annual author and subject indexes. In addition, a separate
group of subject bibliographies is issued by the library on a
regular basis, compiled from listings that have appeared in
Personnel Literature.
ONLINE: No

84. *Personnel Management Abstracts.* Ann Arbor, MI: Univer-
    sity of Michigan, Graduate School of Business Adminis-
    tration. 1955-

The quarterly *Abstracts* is quite a useful tool as its
coverage is broader than its title suggests, with its attention
to related subjects such as organizational behavior. Each issue
is in two sections. The first of these is an index to management literature, from approximately 70 journals. This section
is arranged by 44 subject headings, with each entry receiving
a one- to two-sentence annotation. Author and title indexes
to this section are included. The second half of each issue
is devoted to a selection of lengthier abstracts, of some
titles included in the first section, and with some books added as well. There are no annual cumulations of the indexes.
ONLINE: No

85. *Work Related Abstracts.* Detroit, MI: Information
    Coordinators, Inc. 1950- Former titles: *Labor Per-
    sonnel Index*, 1950-57; *Employment Relations Abstracts*,
    1958-72.

This is another valuable personnel index. It "extracts
the significant, and the informative from over two hundred and
fifty management, labor, government, professional, and university periodicals." Dissertations are also included though
regular monographs are not. The abstracts are issued in monthly inserts, divided into twenty broad subject categories. A
large number of public personnel concerns are regularly covered. The detailed Subject Index appears monthly and cumulates
quarterly and annually. A comprehensive list of *W.R.A.* subject
headings is published bi-annually.
ONLINE: No

86. *Psychological Abstracts.* Washington, DC: American
    Psychological Association. 1927-

An essential abstracting service, providing "nonevalu-
ative summaries of the world's literature in psychology and
related disciplines." Included as part of this literature
are numerous publications dealing with a broad spectrum of organizational and personnel concerns. Each monthly issue is
arranged into sixteen major subject groupings, which are in
turn further sub-divided. The subject section "Applied Psychology" is the most relevant, as its sub-groups include "Personnel selection and training," "Personnel evaluation and performance," "Management and management training," and "Organizational behavior and job satisfaction." A "brief subject
index" and an author index appear in each issue. Comprehen-

sive author and subject indexes appear in June and December. A commercial publisher has issued cumulative author and subject indexes, in various sequences, covering the years 1927-1977. ONLINE: LIS

87. *Labor Literature*. Washington, DC: U. S. Department of Labor, Library. 1976-

Subtitled "Recent additions to the Department of Labor Library," this is a marginally useful tool. The bi-weekly issues are arranged in three parts. A "Books and pamphlets" section is sub-arranged by a variety of subject descriptors. The "Partial contents of selected recent periodicals" listing is arranged alphabetically by journal title and provides abstracts of one or more articles. There is also a subject index to the periodical articles which have been abstracted. ONLINE: No

SOCIAL SERVICES/HEALTH CARE ADMINISTRATION SOURCES

Health care administrators are fortunate in the variety of bibliographic choices available to them, all of which emphasize the non-clinical aspects of management and policy in the medical world.

88. *Index Medicus* (New Series). Bethesda, MD: National Library of Medicine. 1960-

Comprehensive though non-exhaustive coverage of the world's medical literature is provided by *Index Medicus*. Journals and selected monographs in all languages are indexed. Clinical aspects of medical care receive primary emphasis but a substantial amount of material pertaining to health care management topics is included. Primary arrangement of each monthly issue is by subject, with a separate author section also included. Abstracts are not provided in this index. Contents of the monthly issues are cumulated to comprise the annual *Cumulated Index Medicus*.
ONLINE: LIS, BRS
Note: This index is also available online as part of the National Library of Medicine's MEDLARS system. Additional health planning references are retrievable from the MEDLARS system that are not available in the *Index Medicus* data base from LIS and BRS.

89. *Excerpta Medica*. Section 17: Public Health, Social Medicine, and Hygiene. 1955- Section 36: Health Economics and Hospital Management. 1971- Amsterdam, Netherlands: Excerpta Medica.

   Excerpta Medica and *Index Medicus* (Item 88) are the two
major indexing services for the biomedical sciences. The former title is a collection of 43 separate abstracting journals,
two of which are of primary interest here. Organization of
both sections is similar. The high-quality abstracts are
arranged by subject, in a decimalized sequence. Only the journal literature is covered. Separate author and detailed subject indexes are included in each of ten issues per year.
These indexes are cumulated in the last issue of each volume.
Section 17 focuses on all aspects of public health, as indicated by some of the major section headings: general aspects,
statistics, communicable diseases, social hygiene, sanitation,
nutrition, and developing countries. In Section 36 the emphasis
is on the economic and managerial aspects of health care, with
particular focus on hospital management and organization.
ONLINE: LIS
Note: The online version of *Excerpta Medica* contains approximately 40% more references than are listed in the printed abstracts journals.

   90. *Hospital Literature Index*. Chicago: American Hospital
       Association. 1945- Continues: *Hospital Periodicals
       Literature Index*, 1945-1956.

   Non-clinical aspects of medicine and patient care are
emphasized in this essential tool. All administrative aspects
of the delivery of health care are included. Appropriate
articles from journals outside the health field are included.
No books are indexed. Each quarterly issue is arranged by
subject and then sub-arranged by journal title under each subject heading. An author index is provided. A selection of
books acquired by the A.H.A.'s library is listed topically in
a "Recent Acquisitions" section. The final issue of each year
is the annual cumulation. Five-year cumulations are available
for the period 1945-1974 and a three-year cumulation for 1975-
1977.
ONLINE: MEDLARS; LIS, see also the ONLINE citation for Item 88.

   91. *Hospital Abstracts*. London: H.M.S.O. 1961-

   Prepared by the British Department of Health and Social
Security, this monthly publication "aims to cover the whole
field of hospitals and their administration, with the exception
of strictly medical and related professional matters." The
geographical coverage of the listings is worldwide. Most listings are for English language materials; the abstracts are in
English when the original is not. Both monographs and journal
articles are included. Each issue is arranged under a broad
array of hospital-functional subject headings. A separate

subject index also appears in each issue. Unfortunately, there
are no cumulations of the monthly subject indexes.
ONLINE: No

92. *Abstracts of Health Care Management Studies.* Ann Arbor,
    MI: Health Administration Press. 1965- Former title:
    Abstracts of Hospital Management Studies, 1965-1978.

   The invaluable bibliographic aid is published for the
Cooperative Information Center for Health Care Management
Studies at the University of Michigan. It is notable both for
its depth of coverage and for the quality of its abstracts.
Included in its scope are books, articles, dissertations, and
numbered technical reports. Each annual issue is arranged by
46 general subject categories, with separate author and title
indexes. Prior to the 1981 issue this was a quarterly publication, with annual cumulations.
ONLINE: No

93. *MEDOC: A Computerized Index to U. S. Government
    Documents in the Medical and Health Science.* Salt Lake
    City: University of Utah, Spencer S. Eccles Health
    Sciences Library. 1968-

   MEDOC is a very useful tool for accessing U. S. government publications in the health field, as it provides a more
convenient, comprehensive, and subject-specific format than is
available with the *Monthly Catalog* (Item 41). The majority
of the citations are to non-clinical writings, with many administrative, legislative, and planning issues addressed. All
issues are arranged in four parts: document number index
(Supt. of Documents number); title index; subject index; and
series number index. It is necessary to refer to the document
number index from the other three to locate the full bibliographic citation. A helpful feature is the inclusion of price
information, where applicable. Published quarterly, each issue
supersedes the preceding one, with the year's last issue being
the annual cumulative volume. A combined cumulation, covering 1968-1974, has also been published.
ONLINE: BRS

94. *Medical Care Review.* Ann Arbor, MI: Health Administra-
    tion Press. 1967- Continues: *Public Health Economics
    and Medical Care Abstracts,* 1944-1967.

   The journal emphasizes "the reporting of scholarly work
as well as commissioned state of the art review papers." A
highly selective section of abstracts of "publications on medical care organization, finance, and related concerns" is inclu-

ded in each quarterly issue. An annual index to authors and
subjects is issued.
ONLINE: No

95. *Journal of Health Politics, Policy and Law*, "Biblio-
     graphy." Durham, NC: Duke University, Department of
     Health Administration. 1976-

A separate "Bibliography" section appears at the back
of most quarterly issues of this important journal. It is
noted here because of its policy focus and its excellent coverage of non-health care journals, such as law reviews. Arrangement of the section is by 7-9 topical headings. Only journal
articles are listed.
ONLINE: No

96. *Topics in Strategic Planning for Health Care*. New York:
     Haworth Press. 1978- Former title: *Health and Medical
     Care Services Review*.

A modest but useful quarterly publication which is
highly selective in its indexing coverage. Issues have
included review essays on single topics as well as "capsule
summaries" from the current journal literature. The summaries are arranged by title of the journal and only selected
articles are summarized. The literature summarized is non-
clinical, emphasizing services, policy, planning, and administrative aspects.
ONLINE: No

97. *Bibliography of Bioethics*. Detroit, MI: Gale Research
     Company. 1975-

Since health care administration is not a value-free
enterprise, there is considerable worth in this and the following title. "Bioethics can be defined as the systematic study
of value questions which arise in the biomedical and behavioral fields." This bibliography seeks to be comprehensive for
English language publications in all media forms. Arrangement
of the work is by subject, with the headings derived from the
"Bioethics Thesaurus" included in each volume. No abstracts
are provided but a variety of subject descriptors are used to
annotate each entry. Author and title indexes are also provided. Published annually, the bibliography is a product of
an ongoing research project of the Kennedy Institute of the
Center for Bioethics at Georgetown University.
ONLINE: MEDLARS, where a separate Bioethics file is available
as part of the MEDLARS data base.

98. *Bibliography of Society, Ethics and the Life Sciences.*
     Hastings-on-Hudson, NY: Institute of Society, Ethics,
     and the Life Sciences. 1975–

This modest annual publication is selective in its
coverage of books and articles. Entries are partially annotated and are arranged in broad subject sections. Particularly
relevant is the section on "Health Care Delivery," itself sub-
divided into 13 sub-sections. Other sections within the bibliography are also of potential interest. An author index is
included. Each edition of this work updates the previous one
in cumulative, though not inclusive, form.
ONLINE: No
Note: See also the listing for the *NTIS Abstracts Newsletters*
(Item 46), particularly "Health Planning and Health Services
Research."

URBAN ADMINISTRATION SOURCES

Urban affairs/urban planning is closely related to public
administration, particularly at the local government level; thus
the value of the titles noted here.

99. *Urban Affairs Abstracts.* Washington, DC: National
     League of Cities. 1971–

Published jointly by the National League of Cities and
the United States Conference of Mayors, this is both an excep-
tionally useful and usable publication. While its general focus
is the urban environment, this is very broadly defined to include a broad range of public policy issues and concerns.
Only periodicals are surveyed for abstracting. Each issue is
arranged under some 50 topical headings. The actual abstracts
are unusually detailed. Another positive feature is the extensive coverage provided for municipal league publications.
Issued weekly with semi-annual and annual cumulations. The
cumulations include author and geographic indexes.
ONLINE: No

100. *Sage Urban Studies Abstracts.* Beverly Hills, CA:
     Sage Publications, Inc. 1973–

Very similar in format and arrangement to *Sage Public
Administration Abstracts* (Item 53). Public administration
related materials included have a definite urban focus.
Published quarterly.
ONLINE: No

101. *Human Resources Abstracts.* Beverly Hills, CA: Sage
     Publications, Inc. 1966– Former title: *Poverty and
     Human Resources,* 1966–74.

     Another Sage publication, again similar to those cited
above (Items 53 and 100). This title provides "a comprehensive
source of information relating to the problems facing our cities
and nation ... covers human, social and manpower problems and
solutions ranging from slum rehabilitation and job development
training to compensatory education, minority group problems,
and rural poverty."
ONLINE: No

102. *Housing and Planning References.* Washington, DC: U. S.
     Dept. of Housing and Urban Development Library. 1948–
     Former title: *Housing References,* 1948–1960. Issuing
     agency has varied.

     This bibliography is not restricted to housing and
planning listings but also includes a broad range of other
concerns relevant to local government. Books, some government
documents, planning reports, and journal articles are indexed
under approximately 190 subject headings. Single-sentence
annotations are provided for many of the entries. Published
bi-monthly, with geographic and author indexes in each issue.
There are no cumulations.
ONLINE: No

103. *Compendium of Research Reports.* Washington, DC:
     U. S. Dept. of Housing and Urban Development. 1979–

     A semi-annual publication, produced by HUD USER, a
research information service within H.U.D.'s Office of Policy
Development and Research. HUD USER "acquires, summarizes,
and disseminates reports resulting from PDR's extensive research." Each *Compendium* is divided into 50 subject sections,
containing full bibliographic information and quite detailed
abstracts. Indexes are provided for titles, document numbers,
corporate and personal authors, and subjects. Expectedly, the
emphasis of most reports listed is on housing related topics.
A variety of management and policy issues is also studied,
including evaluation, productivity, finance, and local government.
ONLINE: No

3.
professional journals in
public affairs and administration

3. PROFESSIONAL JOURNALS IN
PUBLIC AFFAIRS AND PUBLIC ADMINISTRATION

Richard A. Loverd
Thomas J. Pavlak
Molly M. Wong

Historically, professional journals have served as a primary means of communication for academicians, students and practitioners in public administration. At present, there are scores of periodicals serving the field, hundreds if the scope of public administration is defined quite broadly. Each one seeks to meet what its editors consider to be a special need within the larger field of public administration; each represents a particular conceptual approach, seeks a specific audience of readers, and serves, at least potentially, as a valuable information resource.

This chapter presents an annotated directory of nearly 250 journals in the field of public affairs and administration. Those selected for inclusion were chosen to introduce the reader to the most important and useful of the current English language journals. They also reflect the strong multidisciplinary nature of public affairs and administration as an area of study. Thus, in addition to including periodicals representing the most significant publications in the field (such as *Public Administration Review*, *Public Personnel Management* and *Public Finance Quarterly*), we also sought to include a host of journals from a wide variety of related academic disciplines and professional fields (such as the *American Economic Review*, *Social Service Review* and *Public Works*).

In the entries that follow, those journals deemed most significant are listed under the heading of "Core Journals" (Items 104-131) while those considered supplementary are listed under thirteen specializations:

> Administration and Society (Items 132-181)
> American Government (Items 182-189)
> American Public Administration and Management
> (Items 190-206)

Comparative, Development and International
  Administration (Items 207-239)
Education Administration (Items 240-245)
Environmental Management (Items 246-253)
Justice/Law Enforcement Administration
  (Items 254-260)
Organization Theory and Behavior (Items 261-273)
Public Finance (Items 274-278)
Public Personnel Administration (Items 279-296)
Public Policy and Regulation (Items 297-312)
Social Services/Health Care Administration
  (Items 313-332)
Urban Administration (Items 333-348)

The designation of "Core Journals" was not an easy one.
In a sense, almost all could lay claim to being a part of the
center of public affairs and administration. Considerable
help was provided by a recent study that ranked the prestige
of 41 journals in the field.[1] A number of those periodicals
have been included in the core list.

Each entry provides:

Journal title
Date of origin
Number of issues per year
Whether the journal contains an annual or
  cumulative index
Editor's name and mailing address
A brief description of the journal

In addition, the following manuscript information, derived
from our questionnaire survey of journal editors in 1979-1980
and useful for potential contributors to the journals, is
found in most of the annotations:

Who decides which manuscripts are accepted for
  publication;
The period of time it takes for an editorial
  decision on a manuscript;
After an editorial decision is made, the time
  it takes to publish the manuscript;
The percentage of manuscripts accepted for
  publication.[2] This material is gathered from
  our 1980 survey of the journal editors.

While this chapter was prepared as a comprehensive
guide to journals in public affairs and administration, the
dynamic nature of the field assures that no directory can be
truly comprehensive. As noted in Chapter 1, new journals
are launched each year; some established journals shift their
editorial stance, while others merge with kindred publications,
and some simply cease publication. Still, the periodicals

presented in the pages that follow represent quite strikingly the richness and diversity of public affairs and administration as a field of study, and serve as a useful entry into that vast body of literature.

NOTES

1. Thomas Vocino and Robert H. Elliott, "Journal Prestige in Public Administration," *Administration and Society*, 14 (May 1982), pp. 5-14. Also consult James S. Bowman and Sami G. Hajjar, "English Language Journals in Public Administration: An Analysis," *Public Administration* (Great Britain), 56 (Summer 1978), 203-225 and Harry W. Reynolds, Jr., ed., "Making the Case for a New Public Administration Journal: A Symposium," *American Review of Public Administration*, 15 (Spring 1981), 53-74.

2. It should be noted that responses obtained from these questions were not always as precise as one might have wished. In instances of imprecision, the information provided by the journal editors was interpreted as accurately as possible.

I. CORE JOURNALS

104. *Administration and Society*. 1968. 4. Index. Gary L. Wamsley. Center for Public Administration and Policy, Virginia Polytechnic Institute and State University, Blacksburg, Virginia 24061.

   Administration and Society is a scholarly journal that focuses primarily on empirical research reports and theoretically specific articles dealing with public and human service organizations, their administrative processes, and their effect on society. Its particular interests include the effects of administrative strategies, programs, change interventions, and training; and intergroup, interorganizational and organization-environment relationships and policy processes. Refereed by academics; 2 months for editorial decision; 4-5 months to publish; 55% acceptance for publication.

105. *Administrative Law Review*. 1949. 4. Index. John H. Reese. 200 W. 14th Avenue, Denver, Colorado 80204.

   Sponsored by the Administrative Law Section of the American Bar Association, *ALR* is intended primarily for practicing attorneys, judges, legal scholars and students. It publishes scholarly works and commentaries on all aspects of administrative law, including new legislation, major court rulings, developments in the field, and quantitative and qualitative evaluations of administrative law practices and procedures. Managing Editor decides; 1 month for editorial decision; 4 months to publish; 60% accepted for publication.

106. *Administrative Science Quarterly*. 1956. 4. Index. Karl E. Weick. Graduate School of Business and Public Administration, Cornell University, Ithaca, New York 14853.

ASQ is one of the most prestigious scholarly journals in the field. Intended for researchers and advanced graduate students, it publishes theoretical and empirical analyses dealing with organizational and administrative behavior from both the macro- and the micro-level perspectives. Refereed by academics; 3 months for editorial decision; 6 months to publish; 10% accepted for publication.

107. *American Review of Public Administration* (formerly the *Midwest Review of Public Administration*). 1967. 4. Index. Jerzy Hauptmann. Park College, Parkville, Missouri 64152.

This quarterly journal, for scholars and practitioners, is devoted to current issues of public administration viewed from the field (especially the Midwest) rather than from the nation's capital. Editor decides; 6-9 months for editorial decision; 3-6 months to publish; 25% accepted for publication.

108. *The Annals of the American Academy of Political and Social Science*. 1889. 6. Index. Richard D. Lambert. American Academy of Political and Social Science, 3937 Chestnut St., Philadelphia, Pennsylvania 19104.

The *Annals* is a bi-monthly publication of the Academy, containing articles dealing with some prominent social or political problem, written by authors at the invitation of the editors.

109. *Bureaucrat*. 1972. 4. Thomas Novotny. P. O. Box 5007, Alexandria, Virginia 22305.

The *Bureaucrat* is a practitioner-oriented quarterly journal publishing essays written for the professional public manager and dealing with a broad range of public management issues. Refereed by academics and practitioners; 1½ months for editorial decision; 6 months to publish; 33% accepted for publication.

110. *Comparative Urban Research.* 1972. 3. William John Hanna. University of Maryland, College Park, Maryland 20742.

CUR is a journal for urban scholars and practitioners, dealing with theoretical and methodological issues in urban research, with an emphasis on cross-national and interdisciplinary work. Its articles focus on research relating to cities, metropolitan areas, urbanization, and cross-cultural comparison. Refereed by academics and practitioners; 3 months for editorial decision; 6 months to publish; 25% accepted for publication.

111. *Government Publications Review.* 1973. 4 and 6. Index. Cum. Ind. Bernard M. Fry. Graduate Library School, Indiana University, Bloomington, Indiana 47401.

This publication, intended for librarians, researchers, scholars, and others interested in government information and publications, covers library science, archival management, history, public administration, political science, and sociology. This journal is divided into two parts: Part A (bimonthly) contains scholarly articles and regular features; Part B (quarterly) is a selection tool and alerting service for documents across levels of government. Refereed by academics and practitioners; 1½ months for editorial decision; 6-12 months to publish; 80% accepted for publication.

112. *Harvard Business Review.* 1922. 6. Index. Cum. Ind. Kenneth R. Andrews. Soldiers Field, Boston, Massachusetts 02163.

A publication of the Harvard Business School, *HBR*'s audience includes top management in the United States and abroad, policy-making executives in government and non-commercial organizations, and other professionals interested in the viewpoint of business management. It publishes articles on a broad range of management topics, from accounting to world business. Refereed by *HBR* editors; 1-1½ months for editorial decision; 2-5 months to publish; 5% accepted to publish.

113. *Industrial and Labor Relations Review.* 1947. 4. Index. Donald E. Cullen. New York State School of Industrial and Labor Relations, Cornell University, Ithaca, New York 14853.

This journal, for academics, professionals, and practitioners in industrial and labor relations, publishes original research in the areas of labor-management relations, labor organizations, law, marketing, politics, government and in-

dustrial relations, manpower, personnel, organizational behavior, and international and comparative industrial relations.
Refereed by academics and practitioners; 4-6 months for editorial decision; 3-6 months to publish; 15% accepted to publish.

114.   *International Journal Of Government Auditing.* 1974.
       4. Index. John D. Heller. Room 7124, 441 G Street,
       N. W., Washington, D. C. 20548.

       Sponsored by the International Organization of Supreme
Audit Institutions, this quarterly journal publishes articles
for government auditors worldwide, especially those in less
developed countries. Containing a blend of technical and
general articles, the journal focuses on public sector auditing
techniques, training, and organizational aspects of public
audit offices in various countries. Editor decides: 1-1½ months
for editorial decision; 6-9 months to publish; 25% accepted to
publish.

115.   *International Journal of Public Administration.* 1979.
       4. Index. Jack Rabin and Thomas Vocino. Department
       of Government, Auburn University at Montgomery, Mont-
       gomery, Alabama 36117.

       A relatively new journal in the field, *IJPA* publishes
articles on "theoretical concepts and practical applications
of current research." It focuses on national issues in American public administration, with frequent contributions on significant international topics. Refereed by academics and
practitioners; 1½-2½ months for editorial decision; maximum
of 12 months to publish; 15-20% accepted for publication.

116.   *International Review of Administrative Sciences.* 1928.
       4. Index. Cum. Ind. James Sundquist. International
       Institute of Administrative Sciences, Rue de la Charité,
       25, B-1040 Brussels, Belgium.

       This journal, for academics and practitioners world-wide,
publishes articles on public administration and comparative and
international administration. Editor or Assistant Editor
decides; 1-1½ months for editorial decision; 6-12 months to publish; 20-25% accepted for publication.

117.   *National Civic Review.* 1912. 11. Index. Joan A.
       Casey. National Municipal League, 47 E. 68th Street,
       New York, New York 10021.

       The *National Civic Review* is one of the oldest national
publications devoted to the study of issues in state and local
government. Intended for a broad audience of scholars, prac-

titioners, and the informed public, the *Review* publishes articles
on all aspects of state and local government, including taxation
and finance, citizen action and organization, and metropolitan
and regional developments. Editorial Board decides; 2-3 months
for editorial decision; 3-4 months to publish; 50% accepted for
publication.

118. *Policy Studies Journal.* 1972. 8. Index. Stuart Nagel.
     Department of Political Science, University of Illinois,
     Urbana, Illinois 61801.

   The official journal of the Policy Studies Organization,
PSJ is designed to "promote the application of political and
social science to important policy problems" by publishing symposia and non-symposium articles. Policy areas covered in
recent issues include civil liberties, crime, education, energy,
environment, food, health, housing, labor, national defense,
population, poverty, science and transportation problems.
Refereed by academics and practitioners; 1 month for editorial
decision; 2-6 months to publish; 30% accepted for publication.

119. *Public Administration Review.* 1940. 6. Index. Cum.
     Ind. Louis Gawthrop. School of Public and Environment-
     al Affairs, Indiana University, Bloomington, Indiana
     47401.

   PAR is the official journal of the American Society for
Public Administration. The journal's goal is to "advance the
science, processes, and art of public administration and related policy matters." Each issue features a symposium on a
topic of current interest in public administration, along with
additional articles covering all aspects of public administration. Refereed by academics and practitioners; 2 months for
editorial decision; 6-12 months to publish; 5% accepted for
publication.

120. *Public Budgeting and Finance.* 1980. 4. Jesse Burkhead.
     Maxwell School, Syracuse University, Syracuse, N. Y.
     13210.

   Published by the American Association for Budget and
Program Analysis, this quarterly journal relates developments
in financial management to budgetary practice. The journal's
fields include budgeting, financial management, program analysis and evaluation. Refereed by academics and practitioners;
1½ months for editorial decision; undetermined period to publish; % accepted not available.

121. *Public Choice.* 1966. 4-6. Index. Kenneth A. Shepsle.
     Department of Political Science, Washington University,
     St. Louis, Missouri 63130.

     This journal publishes articles on the intersection of
politics and the economy and its effect on private and public
decision-making. It is intended for the academic and business
communities as well as government officials. Refereed by academics; 1-1½ months for editorial decision; 9 months to publish;
12-15% accepted for publication.

122. *Public Finance Quarterly.* 1973. 4. Index. J. Ronnie
     Davis. College of Business and Economics, Western Wash-
     ington University, Bellingham, Washington 98225.

     A scholarly economics journal for the study of the public
sector of the economy, manuscripts are sought which deal with
the positive or normative aspects of government policies at the
federal, state or local levels. Both theoretical and empirical
studies are welcomed. Papers that analyze current issues of
government policy are of particular interest. Refereed by academics and practitioners; 2 months for editorial decision; 3-6
months to publish; 15% accepted for publication.

123. *Public Interest.* 1965. 4. Irving Kristol and Nathan
     Glaser. National Affairs, Inc., 10 East 53rd Street,
     New York, New York 10022.

     Public Interest is a quarterly journal of domestic public
and social policy, viewed from a conservative perspective, and
intended for the informed general reader as well as the special-
ist. Issues typically are organized around one or two central
themes such as Art and Society, Housing Policy, and the American Commonwealth. Editors decide; 1½ months for editorial
decision; 3 months to publish; 5% accepted for publication.

124. *Public Management.* 1920. 12. Index. Elizabeth K.
     Kellar. International City Management Association, 1140
     Connecticut Avenue, N. W., Washington, D. C. 20036.

     This monthly ICMA publication, intended for local govern-
ment managers and the academic community, features short articles
on current issues in city management, including financial management, economic development, employee motivation, productivity
improvement, and labor relations. Editor and staff decide; 1-3
months for editorial decision; 1-3 months to publish; 5-10%
accepted for publication.

125. *Public Personnel Management.* 1972. 6. Index. Kenneth
     A. Fisher. International Personnel Management Associa-
     tion, 1850 K Street, N. W., Suite 870, Washington, D. C.
     20006.

This quarterly publication of the International Personnel Management Association offers critical analyses of current concepts, systematic examinations of practical problems and solutions, exploration of areas in which further research is needed, and reports on distinctive practices which suggest new directions in personnel management and administration in the public sector. Refereed by academics and practitioners; 4 months for editorial decision; 3 months to publish; 20% accepted for publication.

126. *Public Productivity Review.* 1975. 4. Index. B. F. Krueger. Center for Productive Public Management, John Jay College of Criminal Justice, 445 West 59th Street, New York, New York 10019.

Public Productivity Review focuses on the need to create "a more serious and detailed understanding" of public sector productivity, public administration, management and supervision, and technological innovation. It covers all public sector services and is intended for public sector managers, policy makers, and the academic community. Refereed by academics and practitioners; 1-1½ months for editorial decision; maximum 12 months to publish; 30% accepted for publication.

127. *Public Welfare.* 1943. 4. Index. Bill Detweiler. American Public Welfare Association, 1125 15th Street, N. W., Washington, D. C. 20005.

This quarterly publication of the American Public Welfare Association is "committed to covering every aspect of the welfare field and related areas." Articles analyze national social policy issues, report on significant work in the field, examine social work theory and social legislation, and present ideological points of view from carefully studied positions. Editor decides; 3 months for editorial decision; 3-6 months to publish; 8% accepted for publication.

128. *Science.* 1880. 52. Index. Philip H. Abelson. American Association for the Advancement of Science, 1515 Massachusetts Ave., N. W., Washington, D. C. 20005.

As a weekly journal of the American Association for the Advancement of Science, it seeks to "further the work of scientists, facilitate cooperation among them, foster scientific freedom and responsibility, improve the effectiveness of science in the promotion of human welfare and increase public understanding and appreciation of the importance and promise of the methods of science in human progress." It wishes to serve as a forum for the discussion of important issues related to the advancement of science, including minority or conflicting points of view.

Refereed by academics and practitioners; 10-15 weeks for editorial decision and publication; 20% accepted for publication.

129. *Social Policy.* 1970. 5. Frank Riessman and Colin Greer.
     Social Policy Corporation, 33 West 42nd Street, Room 1212,
     New York, New York 10036.

     This journal, for academics, activists and the general
     public, publishes articles related to contemporary social thought
     and public affairs. Special issues have been devoted to a
     variety of human service topics, including self-help, the elderly,
     health, community organizing, mental health, and education
     assessment. Editors decide; 1 week-1 month for editorial
     decision; 6-12 months to publish; 60% accepted for publication.

130. *Southern Review of Public Administration.* 1977. Index.
     Cum. Ind. Jack Rabin and Thomas Vocino. Department of
     Government, Auburn University at Montgomery, Montgomery,
     Alabama 36117.

     The *Review* is designed to "bridge the gap" between
     academics and practitioners in public management. It contains
     single articles and symposia on major issues in all areas of
     contemporary public administration. Refereed by academics and
     practitioners; 1½ months for editorial decision; maximum 12
     months to publish; 25% accepted for publication.

131. *Urban Affairs Quarterly.* 1965. 4. Index. Louis H.
     Masotti. Northwestern University, 2040 Sheridan Road,
     Evanston, Illinois 60201.

     This quarterly journal for urban scholars, public officials, and city planners seeks to "facilitate the interchange
     of ideas and concerns between those engaged in basic or applied
     urban research and those responsible for making or implementing
     public policy and programs." Its articles deal with all areas
     of urban research, including neighborhood, city, suburban, and
     metropolitan area concerns. Refereed by academics and practitioners; 2-3 months for editorial decision; 12 months to publish;
     14% accepted for publication.

II. ADMINISTRATION AND SOCIETY

132. *American Economic Review.* 1911. 4. Index. Cum. Ind.
     Robert W. Clower. *AER* Editorial Office, University of
     California at Los Angeles, Los Angeles, California 90024.

     AER is the official publication of the American Economic
     Association, an organization dedicated to "the encouragement of

economic research, especially the historical and statistical
study of the actual conditions of industrial life." Each issue
contains several lead articles and shorter papers on a variety
of economic subjects. Refereed by academics and practitioners;
1½-2 months for editorial decision; 6 months to publish; 17%
accepted for publication.

133. *American Journal of Economics and Sociology*. 1941. 4.
     Index. Will Lissner. 50 East 69th Street, New York,
     New York 10021.

This scholarly journal was established to promote empirical research employing an interdisciplinary approach to
problems of the economy and society. It publishes empirical
studies of practical problems in any of the social sciences and
in social philosophy. Refereed by academics and practitioners;
1-3 months for editorial decision; minimum 12 months to publish;
20% accepted for publication.

134. *American Journal of Political Science*. 1957. 4. Index.
     Herb Asher and Herb Weisberg. Department of Political
     Science, Ohio State University, Columbus, Ohio 43210.

Sponsored by the Midwest Political Science Association,
this quarterly scholarly journal publishes empirical articles
on a variety of subjects in political science, with an emphasis
on American politics. Refereed by academics; 1½ months for
editorial decision; 9 months to publish; 12% accepted for publication.

135. *American Journal of Sociology*. 1895. 6. Index.
     Cum. Ind. Edward O. Laumann. The University of Chicago
     Press, 1130 East 59th Street, Chicago, Illinois 60637.

Since its inception in 1895, the *American Journal of
Sociology* has been a leading scholarly publication in social
science research and analysis. It publishes sociological and
interdisciplinary work on the theory, methods, practice and
history of sociology and related fields such as political
sociology, social psychology, demography and the sociology of
education. Refereed by academics and practitioners; 3-4 months
for editorial decision; 7-9 months to publish; 9% accepted for
publication.

136. *American Political Science Review*. 1907. 4. Index.
     Cum. Ind. Dina A. Zinnes. Department of Political
     Science, University of Illinois, Urbana, Illinois 61801.

The official journal of the American Political Science
Association, the *APSR* publishes major theoretical and empirical

papers in all fields of political science, including political
theory, American government, comparative politics, and international politics. Refereed by academics and practitioners; 1-3
months for editorial decision; 6-9 months to publish; 12%
accepted for publication.

137. *American Politics Quarterly*. 1973. 4. Index. Samuel
     A. Kirkpatrick. Department of Political Science, Texas
     A & M University, College Station, Texas 77843.

   American Politics Quarterly is devoted to "the advancement of basic research in all areas of American government--
urban, state, and national." Its articles cover topics such
as public opinion, political parties, political theory, legislative behavior, legal process, administrative organizations,
and intergovernmental relations. Refereed by academics; 3
months for editorial decision; 6 months to publish; 12-15%
accepted for publication.

138. *American Psychologist*. 1946. 12. Index. Charles A.
     Kiesler. American Psychological Association, 1200
     Seventeenth Street, N. W., Washington, D. C. 20036.

   This monthly journal is the official publication of the
American Psychological Association. It publishes articles regarding the relationship of psychology to and with the larger
society, as well as the status and development of diverse fields
of application of psychological knowledge and method. Refereed
by academics and practitioners; 3 months for editorial decision;
10 months to publish; 15% accepted for publication.

139. *American Sociological Review*. 1936. 6. Index.
     Cum. Ind. William H. Form. Department of Sociology,
     University of Illinois, Urbana, Illinois 61801.

   Sponsored by the American Sociological Association, the
ASR publishes scholarly work in the general field of sociology,
including new theoretical developments, methodological innovations, and results of research on fundamental social processes.
Refereed by academics and practitioners; 2-3 months for editorial decision; 6 months to publish; 12% accepted for publication.

140. *Annals of Public and Co-operative Economy*. 1908. 4.
     International Center of Research and Information on Pub-
     lic and Cooperative Economy (CIRIEC), Quai de Rome, 45,
     4000, Liège, Belgium.

   This quarterly publication, intended for scholars and
public sector managers, features research on economic sectors
and their activities, including economic action by public

authorities, national and regional planning, public enterprise, cooperation, self-management, and the role of trade unions in the economic field. Refereed by academics; 1-2 months for editorial decision; publication depends on program of special issues; 56% accepted for publication.

141. *Annals of Regional Science.* 1967. 3. Cum. Ind.
Michael K. Mischaikow. Western Washington University, Bellingham, Washington 98225.

This journal of "urban, regional, and environmental research and policy" is oriented toward problem-solving articles of an interdisciplinary nature. The *Annals* publishes current research ranging over a variety of areas, including urbanization and metropolitan growth; land use patterns and planning; comparative urban systems; transportation studies; municipal services and facilities; regional development and planning; state and municipal finance; resource management and conservation; and energy issues and policy. Refereed by academics and practitioners; 3-4 months for editorial decision; 3-4 months to publish; 30-40% accepted for publication.

142. *Behavioral Science.* 1956. 6. Index. Cum. Ind.
James G. Miller. Systems Science Publications, University of Louisville, Louisville, Kentucky 40208.

This bi-monthly publication, sponsored by the General Systems Science Foundation, reports on systems science and interdisciplinary behavioral research for an audience of systems scientists and interdisciplinary scholars and researchers. Refereed by academics and practitioners; 6-9 months for editorial decision; 4 months to publish; 25% accepted for publication.

143. *Behavioral Science Research.* 1965. 4. Cum. Ind.
Raoul Naroll. Department of Anthropology, State University of New York, Buffalo, New York 14260.

Sponsored by the Human Relations Area Files (HRAF), this quarterly journal of comparative studies publishes articles dealing with comparative methods in anthropology, political science, economics, psychology, geography, sociology, linguistics, and folklore. It also publishes ethnographic bibliographies and HRAF documentation. Refereed by academics and practitioners; 6-8 months for editorial decision; 12-18 months to publish; 50% accepted for publication.

144. *Communication Research.* 1974. 4. Index. F. G. Kline.
School of Journalism and Mass Communications, University of Minnesota, Minneapolis, Minnesota 55455.

Communication Research is a quarterly journal for communication research specialists, publishing interdisciplinary studies of interpersonal and mass communication. Refereed by academics and practitioners; 6 months for editorial decision; 6-12 months to publish; 80% accepted for publication.

145. *Comparative Political Studies*. 1968. 4. Index. Ted Robert Gurr. Department of Political Science, Northwestern University, Evanston, Illinois 60201.

This is an academic journal for scholars and students of comparative politics. It publishes theoretical and empirical research articles dealing with cross-national comparisons of political systems, institutions, processes, and behavior. Refereed by academics; 3-6 months for editorial decision; 6-9 months to publish; 25-30% accepted for publication.

146. *Comparative Politics*. 1968. 4. Index. Dankwart A. Rustow. Graduate Center, The City University of New York, 33 West 42nd Street, New York, New York 10036.

This international journal for scholars and government officials contains articles devoted to comparative analysis of political institutions and behavior. Articles range from political patterns of emerging nations to contrasts in the structure of established societies. Refereed by academics; 3 months for editorial decision; 9-12 months to publish; 25% acceptance for publication.

147. *Feminist Studies*. 1969. 3. Editorial Collective. Women's Studies, University of Maryland, College Park, Maryland 20742.

Feminist Studies is an interdisciplinary academic journal for persons interested in feminist issues and theory. It publishes analytic responses and articles on all areas of research, criticism, and speculation on feminist issues. Refereed by academics; 4 months for editorial decision; 6 months to publish; 10-15% accepted for publication.

148. *Futures*. 1968. 6. Index. Ralph Jones. IPC Science and Technology Press, Ltd., P. O. Box 63, Westbury House, Bury Street, Guilford, GU2 5BH, England.

Futures is an international journal of planning and forecasting, intended for an audience of decision-makers and planners in government, industry and the academic world. Its articles cover all aspects of the methods and practice of long-term forecasting. Refereed by academics and practitioners; 2 months for editorial decision; 4 months to publish; % accepted not available.

149. *Futurics.* 1976. 4. Index. Scott W. Erickson. Future
     Systems, Inc., Suite 207, 1422 W. Lake Street, Minneapo-
     lis, Minnesota 55408.

   An interdisciplinary journal for researchers, educators,
public administrators and corporate executives, *Futurics* seeks
to facilitate the communication of ideas exploring alternative
futures and to promote the development and understanding of
methods for the study of the future. Refereed by academics
and practitioners; 3-6 months for editorial decision; 6 months
to publish; 25-30% accepted for publication.

150. *Futurist.* 1966. 6. Index. Cum. Ind. Edward Cornish.
     4916 St. Elmo Avenue, Washington, D. C. 20014.

   Sponsored by the World Future Society, the *Futurist*
appeals to a broad audience of persons interested in various
aspects of the future. Articles explore all aspects of the
future, including life-styles, technology, government, economics, environmental affairs, values, and religion. Editor
decides; time for editorial decision varies; 2-6 months to
publish; 10% accepted for publication.

151. *Growth and Change: A Journal of Regional Development.*
     1970. 4. Index. Charles Hultamn. College of
     Business and Economics, University of Kentucky, 644
     Maxwelton Court, Lexington, Kentucky 40506.

   This interdisciplinary journal for academics and professionals in regional development presents the policy implications and applied results of research in economics, geography,
regional and urban planning, and political science, as these
are related to regional development. Refereed by academics
and practitioners; 3-4 months for editorial decision; 3-6
months to publish; 20-25% accepted for publication.

152. *International Journal of General Systems.* 1974. 4.
     Index. Cum. Ind. George J. Klir. Department of Systems
     Science, State University of New York, Binghamton,
     New York 13901.

   This international quarterly is devoted primarily to the
publication of original research and educational contributions
relevant to general systems, such as foundations of general
systems theory and methodology; applications of the methodology
in various branches of science, technology, humanities, and the
arts; general systems philosophy; and general systems education.
Articles cover a variety of topics within these areas, including

principles of modeling and simulation; systems analysis and
synthesis; optimization; and studies concerned with various
classes of systems such as self-organizing, adaptive, self-
producing, fuzzy, and hierarchical systems. Refereed by academics and practitioners; 3-6 months for editorial decision;
3-6 months to publish; 20% accepted for publication.

153. *International Studies Quarterly*. 1957. 4. Index.
     P. Terence Hopmann. Harold Scott Quigley Center of
     International Studies, Hubert H. Humphrey Institute of
     Public Affairs, 1246 Social Sciences Building, Univer-
     sity of Minnesota, Minneapolis, Minnesota 55455.

This interdisciplinary journal, primarily for members
of the International Studies Association but also of interest
to researchers, policy-makers, teachers, and students of international affairs, promotes interaction and collaboration among
specialists whose interests are focused upon trans-national
phenomena. It publishes international and cross-national comparative studies, with an emphasis on interdisciplinary approaches. Refereed by academics and practitioners; 2 months
for editorial decision; 6 months to publish; 15% accepted for
publication.

154. *The Journal of Applied Behavioral Science*. 1966. 4.
     Index. Louis A. Zurcher. NTL Institute, P. O. Box 9155
     Rosslyn Station, Arlington, Virginia 22209.

JABS is a journal for behavioral scientists, professional change agents, potential clients of social change agents,
and public policy-makers. It provides a forum for developing
and testing conceptual approaches to planned change, reporting
on social interventions, and evaluating underlying values
inherent in attempts at planned change. Fields covered include
planned social change, organization behavior, small group
theory and practice, applications of social science to public
policy, and case studies in the above areas. Refereed by
academics and practitioners; 2½ months for editorial decision;
6-12 months to publish; 15% accepted for publication.

155. *Journal of Applied Social Psychology*. 1971. 6. Index.
     Siegfried Streufert. Department of Behavioral Science,
     Hershey Medical Center, Pennsylvania State University
     Medical School, Hershey, Pennsylvania 17033.

This bi-monthly journal publishes behavioral science
research having applications to problems of society. Subject
fields included in the journal's articles are social psychology,
political science and law, sociology, behavioral economics and

behavioral medicine. Refereed by academics and practitioners; 1½ months for editorial decision; 2-4 months to publish; 12% accepted for publication.

156. *Journal of Black Studies.* 1970. 4. Index. Molefi Kete Asante. Department of Black Studies, State University of New York, Buffalo, New York 14260.

Featuring scholarly articles on a wide range of social science topics, this quarterly journal provides analytical discussions of issues related to persons of African descent. Refereed by academics; 2 months for editorial decision; minimum 12 months to publish; 18% accepted for publication.

157. *Journal of the Institute for Socioeconomic Studies.* 1976. 4. Index. Cum. Ind. B. A. Rittersporn, Jr. The Institute for Socioeconomic Studies, Airport Road, White Plains, New York 10604.

This quarterly journal publishes articles covering topics relating to the quality of life, economic development, social motivation, poverty, urban regeneration, and the problems of the elderly. Editor and publisher decide; 1 month for editorial decision; 2 months to publish; % accepted not available.

158. *Journal of Political Economy.* 1892. 6. Index. G. J. Stigler. 1126 E. 59th Street, Chicago, Illinois 60637.

The *Journal of Political Economy* publishes analytical, interpretive, and empirical studies of economic theory and practice. Its subject fields include traditional economics (monetary theory, fiscal policy, labor economics, micro- and macro-theory, international trade and finance, and industrial (organization) and interdisciplinary studies, including social economics, history of economic thought, and the application of economic analysis to socio-political behavior. Refereed by academics and practitioners; 2-6 months for editorial decision; 6-8 months to publish; 12% accepted for publication.

159. *Journal of Political and Military Sociology.* 1973. 2. George A. Kourvetaris. Department of Sociology, Northern Illinois University, DeKalb, Illinois 60115.

This bi-annual journal examines political and military issues from a world perspective, including areas such as political and military sociology, political conflict, world conflict, and institutional analyses. It explores the relationship between politics and the armed forces, the role of the military in society, and the impact of society on the military. Refereed by academics and practitioners; 3 months for editorial decision; 6 months to publish; 13-15% accepted for publication.

160. *Journal of Politics*. 1939. 4. Index. Joseph Bernd. Department of Political Science, Virginia Polytechnic Institute and State University, Blacksburg, Virginia 24061.

The official publication of the Southern Political Science Association, the *Journal of Politics* publishes articles and research notes in all areas of political science, including political theory, American government and politics, and comparative politics. Refereed by academics and practitioners; 2 months for editorial decision; 9 months to be published; 10% accepted for publication.

161. *Law and Contemporary Problems*. 1933. 4. Cum. Ind. Mary B. Funk. Duke University School of Law, Durham, North Carolina 27706.

This journal, for judges, lawyers, and the academic community, publishes symposia dealing with legal, economic, administrative and other social science aspects of a range of contemporary problems of society. Recent issues have focused on Desegregation, Changing Rules for Changing Forms of Welfare, the Effects of Regulation on Innovation, and the American Jury. Editor decides; 2 weeks for editorial decision; 12 months to publish; 50% accepted for publication.

162. *Law and Society Review*. 1966. 4. Index. Joel B. Grossman. 7113 Social Science Building, University of Wisconsin, Madison, Wisconsin 53706.

The official journal of the Law and Society Association, this scholarly quarterly publishes theoretical and empirical research on all aspects of the interrelationships of law, the legal system, and society. Refereed by academics; 3 months for editorial decision; publication depends upon current backlog; 10% accepted for publication.

163. *Philosophy and Public Affairs*. 1971. 4. Scotia W. MacRae. Princeton University Press, Princeton, New Jersey 08540.

This interdisciplinary journal provides a forum for philosophical discussion of legal, social and political issues of current concern. Its contributions draw on a number of disciplines, including philosophy, law, political science, economics and sociology. Refereed by academics; 2 months for editorial decision; 6 months to publish; 10% accepted for publication.

164. *Politics and Society.* 1968. 4. Erik Olin Wright. Department of Sociology, University of Wisconsin, Madison, Wisconsin 53706.

This journal publishes theoretical and empirical contributions to Marxist and other critical perspectives on politics in the subject fields of the state and politics, social change and social movements, revolutions, and Marxist theory. It is intended primarily for an audience of academics and critical-left intellectuals. Refereed by academics; 3-4 months for editorial decision; 3-4 months to publish; 10% accepted for publication.

165. *Public Opinion Quarterly.* 1937. 4. Index. Cum. Ind. Eleanor Singer. Graduate School of Journalism, Columbia University, 116th Street and Broadway, New York, New York 10027.

Sponsored by the American Association for Public Opinion Research, *POQ* emphasizes an interdisciplinary approach to the study of public opinion. It is a leading source of information about public opinion and communication research, propaganda, survey methods, and related subjects such as market research and public relations. Refereed by academics and practitioners; 3-5 months for editorial decision; 6-9 months to publish; 10-15% accepted for publication.

166. *Public Works.* 1896. 12. Index. Edward B. Rodie. Public Works Journal Corporation, P. O. Box 688, Ridgewood, New Jersey 07451.

This journal publishes technically oriented articles on all aspects of public works engineering and administration. Its subject fields include streets and highways, traffic control, street lighting, and parking; water supply, treatment and distribution; wastewater collection and treatment; and solid waste collection and disposal. Its intended audience is public works administrators and engineers in cities, counties and states, plus consulting engineers in private practice. Editorial staff decides; 1 week for editorial decision; 4 months to publish; 75% accepted for publication.

167. *Regional Studies.* 1967. Index. Cum. Ind. J. B. Goddard. Center for Urban and Regional Development Studies, Department of Geography, The University, Newcastle on Tyne NE1 7RU, England.

This bi-monthly publication of the Regional Studies Association is intended for an audience of academics and policymakers. Its articles deal with all aspects of regional studies.

Editor decides; 3 months for editorial decision; 5-6 months to
be published; 20% accepted for publication.

168. *Review of Black Political Economy.* 1969. 4. Index.
     Lloyd Hogan. Atlanta University Center, 360 Westview
     Drive, S. W., Atlanta, Georgia, 30310.

     This journal publishes scholarly studies of issues in
black economic development from a black perspective. The only
journal of its kind, the *Review* focuses on articles that have
some applicability to specific politico-economic problems
facing black Americans. Refereed by academics and practitioners; 2 months for editorial decision; 6 months to publish; 60%
accepted for publication.

169. *Review of Public Data Use.* 1972. 4. Cum. Ind.
     Karen Stroup. c/o DUALabs, 1601 N. Kent Street,
     Arlington, Virginia 22209.

     The *Review* is an interdisciplinary journal devoted to
public data access and use. It publishes primary articles and
current awareness information on social science research and
methodology using publicly available data bases. In addition,
its coverage includes planning and research in state and local
government fields, computer software for accessing statistical
data files, technical problems of data access, legislative and
administrative actions affecting public access, and foreign
data use developments. Refereed by academics and practitioners;
3 months for editorial decision; 4 months to publish; 50% accepted for publication.

170. *Self-Reliance.* 1976. 6. David Macgregor. Institute
     for Local Self-Reliance, 1717 18th Street, N. W., Wash-
     ington, D. C. 20036.

     This bi-monthly publication, for practitioners, commu-
nity groups, local and state officials, and the academic
community, features brief articles on research relating to
urban energy systems, waste utilization, local food production,
and community economic development. Editor decides; 1 month
for editorial decision; 1 month to be published; 50% accepted
for publication.

171. *Social Forces.* 1922. 4. Index. Cum. Ind. Everett K.
     Wilson. Department of Sociology, University of North
     Carolina, Chapel Hill, North Carolina 27514.

     Social Forces is a scholarly journal of social research.
Its articles typically are empirical studies set against a back-
drop of relevant theory. Special issues have been devoted to a

broad range of topics, such as Crime and Delinquency, Social
Mobility, and Work and Leisure. Refereed by academics and
practitioners; 2 months for editorial decision; 9 months to
publish; 10-15% accepted for publication.

172. *Social Indicators Research*. 1974. 4. Alex C. Michalos.
     D. Reidel Publishing Co., Box 17, Dordrecht, Netherlands.

An international and interdisciplinary journal, *SIR*
deals with all aspects of quality-of-life measurement. Articles include empirical, philosophical, and methodological
studies of physical and psycho-social conditions contributing
to the quality of human existence, including health, population,
shelter, transportation, natural environment, social customs
and morality, mental health, law enforcement, politics, education, religion, media and the arts, science and technology,
economics, poverty and welfare. Refereed by academics and
practitioners; 2 months for editorial decision; 12-18 months
to publish; 60% accepted for publication.

173. *Social Praxis*. 1973. 4. Index. Cum. Ind. K. T. Fann.
     37 Kingswood Road, Toronto M4E 3N4, Canada.

Social Praxis is an international and interdisciplinary
journal of social thought. It publishes theoretical, empirical,
and critical studies in the fields of philosophy, economics,
political science, and sociology. Refereed by academics; 2
months for editorial decision; 4 months for publication; 30%
accepted for publication.

174. *Social Problems*. 1953. 4. Index. Cum. Ind. Malcolm
     Spector. Department of Sociology, McGill University,
     855 Sherbrooke Street West, Montreal, Q. P. H3A 2T7,
     Canada.

This quarterly is the official journal of the Society
for the Study of Social Problems. As a journal of applied
sociology, it publishes theoretical and empirical articles on
U. S. and international social problems as illuminated by
sociological analysis. Refereed by academics; 2 months for
editorial decision; 3-5 months to publish; 8% accepted for
publication.

175. *Social Research*. 1940. 4. Index. Arien Mack.
     New School for Social Research, 65 Fifth Avenue,
     New York, New York 10003.

Social Research is a quarterly international journal of
political and social science, published for a broad audience of
social scientists and the informed public. Its articles are

drawn primarily from the fields of sociology, philosophy, political theory, economics, psychology and anthropology. Refereed
by academics; 1 week for editorial decision; 2 months to publish;
% accepted not available.

176. *Social Science Journal*. 1962. 3. Index. Cum. Ind.
     S. Stanley Eitzen. Colorado State University, Fort
     Collins, Colorado 80523.

     Sponsored by the Western Social Science Association,
this scholarly journal for academics in the social sciences
publishes articles in anthropology, sociology, political
science, geography, urban affairs, history, and economics.
Refereed by academics; 1½ months for editorial decision; 6-12
months to publish; 15% acceptance for publication.

177. *Social Theory and Practice*. 1970. 3. Rosa L. Kasper.
     Department of Philosophy, The Florida State University,
     Tallahassee, Florida 32306.

     The intended audience for this international and inter-
disciplinary journal is philosophers and anyone interested in
both theoretical and practical issues in social philosophy.
The journal seeks to provide a forum for the discussion of important and controversial social and political issues. Refereed by academics; 4 months for editorial decision; 6-9 months
to be published; 10% accepted for publication.

178. *Technology in Society*. 1979. 4. Index. George Bugli-
     arello and A. George Schillinger. Box 693, Polytechnic
     Institute of New York, 333 Jay Street, Brooklyn, New
     York 11201.

     Technology in Society is an interdisciplinary journal
dealing with topics related to the impact of technology on
society. It is intended for an audience of intellectual lay
readers in government, industry and the academic community.
Refereed by academics and practitioners; 3-6 months for editorial decision; 3 months to publish; 20% accepted for publication.

179. *Technology Review*. 1899. 8. Index. John I. Mattill.
     Massachusetts Institute of Technology, Cambridge,
     Massachusetts 02139.

     Technology Review is a journal for practicing scientists
and engineers and for those concerned with technology policy
and management. It publishes articles dealing with new developments in technology and their implications for human affairs.
Editors and invited critics decide; 1½ months for editorial

decision; no rule for publication date; 20% accepted for publication.

180. *Western Political Quarterly.* 1948. 4. Index.
Dean E. Mann. Department of Political Science, University of California–Santa Barbara, Santa Barbara, California 93106.

A publication of the Western Political Science Association, the *Quarterly* offers a wide range of articles based on
research in the field of political science, aimed toward the
professional political scientist. Refereed by academics and
practitioners; 3 months for editorial decision; 18–24 months to
publish; 7% accepted for publication.

181. *Youth and Society.* 1962. 4. Index. Cum. Ind.
David Gottlieb. 312 PGH Building, University of
Houston Central Campus, Houston, Texas 77004.

Youth and Society is an interdisciplinary journal focusing on the study of the child and youth socialization, with
emphasis on the implications and consequences of findings for
social policy, program development, and institutional functioning. Its subject areas include adolescence; youth; socialization; family; and cross-cultural studies. Refereed by academics and practitioners; 1 month for editorial decision; 6 months
for publication; 17% accepted for publication.

III. AMERICAN GOVERNMENT

182. *Legislative Studies Quarterly.* 1976. 4. Index.
Cum. Ind. Malcolm E. Jewell. Department of Political
Science, University of Kentucky, Lexington, Kentucky
40506.

This is an international journal covering research on
all aspects of legislative bodies, their functions in the political system, and activities of legislators. Emphasis is
placed on the cross-national and comparative aspects of legislative research. Refereed by academics (editorial board,
outside referees); 1½–2½ months for editorial decision; 3–5
months for publication; 33% accepted for publication.

183. *Municipal Management: A Journal.* 1978. 4. Index.
Charles S. Jakiela. 39 Pearl Street, Brandon, Vermont
05733.

Municipal Management is a practitioner-oriented journal
for municipal managers and political leaders in small and

medium-sized communities. It publishes articles on issues of
importance to small-town community leaders, successful community solutions to significant local problems, and the professional development of town and city managers. Refereed by
academics and practitioners; 1½ months for editorial decision;
6-9 months to be published; 60% accepted for publication.

184. *Polity*. 1968. 4. Cum. Ind. Howard J. Wiarda.
      Thompson Hall, University of Massachusetts, Amherst,
      Massachusetts 01003.

      Sponsored by the Northeastern Political Science Asso-
ciation, *Polity* is a general journal for professional political
scientists, publishing articles in all areas of political science, including American government, comparative politics, and
political theory. Refereed by academics; 3 months for editorial decision; 12 months to publish; 15% acceptance for publication.

185. *Presidential Studies Quarterly*. 1971. 4. R. Gordon
      Hoxie. Center for the Study of the Presidency, 926
      Fifth Avenue, New York, New York 10021.

      Intended for a broad audience, *PSQ* is devoted to examin-
ing the American Presidency, historically, presently, and per-
spectively, with emphasis on political processes including
national leadership and relationships with Congress. Refereed
by editor with board of editors; 3 months for editorial decision;
2 months to publish; 35% acceptance rate for publication.

186. *Publius: The Journal of Federalism*. 1971. 4. Index.
      Daniel J. Elazar. Center for the Study of Federalism,
      Galdfelter Hall, Temple University, Philadelphia, Penn-
      sylvania 19122.

      Publius is dedicated to the study of "federal principles,
institutions and processes." It publishes articles on the theoretical and practical dimensions of American federalism and
other federal systems throughout the world. Topics covered
include decentralization, suburbanization, political community,
and policy choice. Refereed by academics and practitioners; 3
months for editorial decision; 6-12 months to publish; 10-15%
accepted for publication.

187. *State Government: The Journal of State Affairs*. 1930.
      4. Index. Jack L. Gardner. The Council of State
      Governments, P. O. Box 11910, Iron Works Pike, Lexington,
      Kentucky 40578.

State Government is aimed at an audience of state government elected and administrative officials, community leaders, educators, and others interested in state government. It contains articles on a wide range of state government problems, programs, procedures, and innovative practices. Articles deal with individual states and with multi-state and interstate affairs. Refereed by academics, practitioners, editor; 1-2 months for editorial decision; 1-2 months to publish; 25% accepted for publication.

188. *State and Local Government Review.* 1976. 3. Cum. Ind.
     C. David Billings. Institute of Government, Terrell
     Hall, University of Georgia, Athens, Georgia 30602.

Intended for an audience of practitioners and academicians interested in local government, the *Review* provides an interchange of ideas on applied research, service, training, and policy-making in state and local government. Refereed by academics and practitioners; 4 months for editorial decision; 15 months to publish; 20% accepted for publication.

189. *State Legislatures.* 1975. 10. Index. Steve Millard.
     National Conference of State Legislatures, 1125 17th
     Street, Suite 1500, Denver, Colorado 80202.

State Legislatures covers political issues relating to the states, such as revenue sharing, energy, tax and spending limits, etc. Its primary audience is state legislators, along with other public officials, lobbyists, and corporate executives. Editor decides; 1 month for editorial decision; 2-4 months to publish; % accepted not available.

IV. AMERICAN PUBLIC ADMINISTRATION AND MANAGEMENT

190. *Academy of Management Journal.* 1958. 4. Index.
     John W. Slocum. Cox School of Business, Southern
     Methodist University, Dallas, Texas 75275.

This quarterly journal, sponsored by the Academy of Management, is intended primarily for an academic audience. It publishes original research on a wide variety of management topics, oriented primarily toward the private sector. Refereed by academics; 1½ months for editorial decision; 15 months to publish; 15% accepted for publication.

191. *Academy of Management Review.* 1976. 4. Index.
     James E. Rosenzweig. Graduate School of Business Administration, University of Washington, DJ-10, Seattle,
     Washington 98195.

Sponsored by the Academy of Management, the *Review* publishes articles in the fields of management history, management education and development, organizational behavior, business policy and planning, managerial consultation, production-operations management, organization and management theory, personnel-human resources, social issues in management, organizational development, organization communication, health care administration, and the public sector. Its articles focus on theoretical and empirical work having clear implications for problem solving and action in organizational situations. Refereed by academics and practitioners; 1½ months for editorial decision; 9-12 months to publish; 20% accepted for publication.

192. *Advanced Management Journal.* 1935. 4. Index.
      Florence Stone. AMACOM, 135 W. 50th Street, New York,
      New York 10020.

Sponsored by the Society for Advancement of Management, this quarterly journal publishes articles on a broad range of management topics designed primarily to aid middle and upper level managers in increasing their knowledge of management developments, and to provide information which can be useful in their own work situations. Editor decides; 1 week for editorial decision; 3 months to decide; 30% accepted for publication.

193. *Business Horizons.* 1958. 6. Index. Harvey Bunke.
      Indiana University School of Business, 625 N. Jordan,
      Bloomington, Indiana 47405.

This journal publishes articles on personnel, organizational planning and design, finance, marketing, international business and other subjects of interest to academics and business managers. Refereed by academics; 6 weeks for editorial decision; 6-12 months to publish; 10-15% accepted for publication.

194. *California Management Review.* 1958. 4. Index.
      David Vogel. 350 Barrows Hall, University of California,
      Berkeley, California 94720.

This publication, for managers and business executives, seeks to serve as a bridge between creative thought about management and executive action. Editor decides; 2 months for editorial decision; 6-9 months to publish; 10% accepted for publication.

195. *Evaluation and Program Planning.* 1978. 4. Index.
Jonathan A. Morell and Eugenie Walsh Flaherty. Hahnemann
Medical College and Hospital, Department of Mental Health
Sciences, Research and Evaluation Service, 112 North
Broad Street, Philadelphia, Pennsylvania 19102.

This interdisciplinary journal seeks to offer evaluators
and program planners innovative solutions to practical problems,
different ways to analyze and interpret data, and improved
methods of integrating evaluation with program planning. It
explores the evaluation and planning programs with social implications conducted by government, industry, and the non-profit
sector. Refereed by academics and practitioners; 3 months for
editorial decision; 3 months to publish; 25% accepted for publication.

196. *Evaluation Review.* 1977. 6. Index. Richard A. Berk
and Howard Freeman. Institute for Social Science Research,
Bunche Hall, University of California, Los Angeles,
California 90024.

This bi-monthly journal, for social scientists and administrators involved in the evaluation of social programs, publishes
articles on applied social science, particularly articles on the
evaluation of social programs. It also publishes research
"briefs" and "craft notes." Refereed by academics and practitioners; 3 months for editorial decision; 6 months to publish;
10% accepted for publication.

197. *Interfaces.* 1970. 6. R. E. Woolsey. Mining Economics
Department, Colorado School of Mines, Golden, Colorado
80401.

Sponsored by the Institute of Managment Sciences/Opera-
tions Research Society of America, this bi-monthly publication
is concerned with the operational problems encountered in utili-
zing and implementing operations research and management science
techniques and is directed primarily at those having managerial
responsibilities and interests. Its articles typically describe
the use or application of OR/MS in business, industry, or government operations, with emphasis on operational problems encountered in implementation. Editor-in-chief decides; 1 month for
editorial decision; 5-8 months to publish; 50% accepted for publication.

198. *Journal of Policy Analysis and Management.* 1981. 4.
Index. Raymond Vernon. The Kennedy School of Government,
Room 346, 79 Boylston Street, Cambridge, Massachusetts
02138.

This is a journal of the social sciences that focuses on the best current work of political scientists, economists, historians, and sociologists--in both the academic world and the public sector--on issues of public policy. It also emphasizes analyses of empirical evidence on the issues. Refereed by academics and practitioners; 2 weeks-2 months for editorial decision; 3 months to publish; 5% accepted for publication.

199. *Journal of Public and International Affairs.* 1978. 2. Index. Olivia Yates. Graduate School of Public and International Affairs, 3R03 Forbes Quadrangle, University of Pittsburgh, Pittsburgh, Pennsylvania 15260.

This bi-annual journal treats issues pertaining to public policy research and analysis on the local, regional, national and international levels, with special emphasis given to interdisciplinary and multidisciplinary approaches. Topics covered include public policy, international affairs, development, urban and regional planning, and public administration. Refereed by academics and practitioners; 4-5 months for editorial decision; 2-8 months to publish; 20% accepted for publication.

200. *Management Review.* 1923. 12. Index. John M. Roach. American Management Association, 135 West 50th Street, New York, New York 10020.

Subtitled "The Magazine for Motivated Managers," this journal is an AMA publication written largely for and by practitioners of management. The articles are short and practical in nature. Editor decides; 2 months for editorial decision; 4 months to publish; 10% accepted for publication.

201. *Management Science.* 1954. 12. Index. Cum. Ind. Martin K. Starr. The Institute of Management Science, 146 Westminster Street, Providence, Rhode Island 02903.

Sponsored by The Institute of Management Sciences (TIMS), *MS* publishes articles primarily of a technical nature for management scientists and managers. Its articles cover a broad range of topics, including finance; production and operations management; research and development; dynamic programming and inventory theory; mathematical programming and its applications; marketing; logistics; network modeling and facility location; decision analysis; information and systems sciences; interactive behavior, effectiveness and design; applied stochastic methods; and planning, forecasting and gaming. Refereed by academics and practitioners; 6 months for editorial decision; 3 months to publish; 15% accepted for publication.

202. *Mathematics of Operations Research*. 1976. 4. Index.
Arthur F. Veinott, Jr. The Institute of Management
Sciences and the Operations Research Society of America,
146 Westminster Street, Providence, Rhode Island 02903.

This quarterly ORSA/TIMS journal publishes research and
review papers having substantial mathematical interest and relevance to operations research and management science. Its subject fields include mathematical programming, stochastic systems, game theory in multi-person decisions, dynamic programming
and control, and combinatorial systems. Refereed by academics
and practitioners; 6 months for editorial decision; 6 months to
publish; 27% accepted for publication.

203. *Operations Research*. 1952. 6. Index. Cum. Ind.
William P. Pierskalla. 2 Denford Drive, Newton Square,
Pennsylvania 19073.

Sponsored by the Operations Research Society of America,
OR is a bi-monthly journal that publishes articles on operations
research as well as on the history, policy, future, and arenas
of application of operations research. Refereed by academics
and practitioners; 4-6 months for editorial decision; 6-12
months to publish; 22-25% accepted for publication.

204. *Review of Business and Economic Research*. 1965. 3.
Index. Jerry P. Simpson. Division of Business and
Economic Research, University of New Orleans, New Orleans,
Louisiana 70122.

This academic journal is devoted to enhancing the understanding of business and economic phenomena, with an emphasis
on accounting, finance, information systems, management, marketing, and quantitative analysis. Refereed by academics;
2 months for editorial decision; 6 months to publish; 20%
accepted for publication.

205. *Simulation and Games*. 1970. 4. Index. Cathy Stein
Greenblat. Department of Sociology, Douglass College,
Rutgers University, New Brunswick, New Jersey 08903.

This journal provides a forum for theoretical and empirical papers related to man, man-machine, and machine simulation of social processes. *Simulation and Games* publishes
theoretical papers about simulation in research and teaching,
empirical studies, and technical papers on new gaming techniques.
Refereed by academics; 2 months for editorial decision; 6 months
to publish; 25% accepted for publication.

206. *Sloan Management Review.* 1960. 4. Index. Cum. Ind.
     Gay Van Ausdall. Sloan Management Review Association,
     50 Memorial Drive, Cambridge, Massachusetts 02139.

The *Review* publishes articles that provide practicing
managers with the latest tools and information needed for
effective problem-solving and decision-making. The majority
of the *Review*'s articles are in the following areas: planning
and control systems; management information systems; organizational studies; finance; managerial economics; marketing;
R & D management; labor relations; and international business.
Refereed by academics and practitioners; 2-4 months for editorial decision; 2-3 months to publish; 15% accepted for publication.

V. COMPARATIVE, DEVELOPMENT AND INTERNATIONAL ADMINISTRATION

207. *Administration for Development.* 1974. 2. S. N. Kenehe.
     Administrative College of Papua New Guinea, P. O. Box 1216,
     Boroko, Papua New Guinea.

This bi-annual journal deals with a broad range of
topics in development administration, with particular reference
to Melanesia.

208. *Administrative Science Review.* 1962. 4. Abdus Sattar
     Khan. National Institute of Public Administration,
     Nilkhet, Dacca - 2, Bangladesh.

This quarterly journal publishes articles dealing with
current topics related to public administration, development
economics, financial administration and rural development, and
is intended for government officials and the academic community.
NIPA editorial board decides; 1 month for editorial decision;
2 months to publish; 80% accepted for publication.

209. *Alternatives: A Journal of World Policy.* 1975. 4.
     Index. Cum. Ind. Saul Mendlovitz. Institute for
     World Order, 777 United Nations Plaza, New York, New
     York 10017.

Alternatives is a quarterly journal for scholars and
policy-makers concerned with world policy issues. It seeks to
provide, from a value-centered perspective, policy-relevant
analyses of major global issues and presents alternative para-
digms, processes and strategies for confronting problems and
ecological deterioration. Refereed by academics and practitioners; 2½-3 months for editorial decision; 3-4½ months to publish;
25-30% accepted for publication.

210. *American Journal of International Law.* 1907. 4. Index.
      Cum. Ind. Oscar Schachter and Louis Henkin. School of
      Law, Columbia University, New York, New York 10027.

The official publication of the American Society of
International Law, this quarterly journal publishes scholarly
articles, commentaries, and selected official documents on
public and private international law, the law of international
organizations, and the foreign relations law of the United
States and other countries. Refereed by academics and practitioners; 2 weeks-1 month for editorial decision; 3 months to
publish; 20% accepted for publication.

211. *Asian Survey.* 1961. 12. Robert A. Scalapino and
      Leo E. Rose. University of California Press, Berkeley,
      California 94720.

Asian Survey is a monthly journal of contemporary Asian
studies, intended for scholars, the business community, and the
informed public. It publishes articles on political, social
and economic developments in Asia. Refereed by academics and
practitioners; 2-3 months for editorial decision; 6-12 months
to publish; 40% accepted for publication.

212. *Australian Journal of Public Administration.* 1937. 4.
      Index. Cum. Ind. G. R. Curnow. Department of Govern-
      ment and Public Administration, University of Sydney,
      Sydney, N. S. W. 2006, Australia.

Sponsored by the Australian Institute of Public Administration, this quarterly journal contains articles on theoretical and practical aspects of public administration in federal,
state and local government in Australia, as well as articles
on developments overseas having implications for Australia.
Editor decides; 1-2 months for editorial decision; 3-9 months
to publish; 45% accepted for publication.

213. *Behavioral Sciences and Rural Development.* 1967. 2.
      Index. Cum. Ind. S. K. Rau. National Institute of
      Rural Development, Rajendranagar, Hyderabad, 500030,
      India.

This bi-annual journal, intended for policy-makers,
administrators, academics, and practitioners involved in rural
development, aims at promoting interdisciplinary study and research in the behavioral sciences concerned with rural development as a concept, a movement, and a program. It publishes
articles on all aspects of the social sciences relating to rural
development. Refereed by academics and practitioners; 6-8
months for editorial decision; 6 months to publish; 20% accepted for publication.

214. *Canadian Public Administration.* 1958. 4. Index.
      Cum. Ind. Kenneth Kernaghan. 897 Bay Street, Toronto,
      Ontario M5S 1Z7, Canada.

      Sponsored by the Institute of Public Administration of
Canada, this quarterly journal is intended for public servants
and academics in Canada and elsewhere. It publishes articles
in the fields of public management, public policy, political
science, economics, social psychology, and urban planning.
Its focus is on articles which examine the structures, processes
and outcomes of public policy and public management related to
executive, legislative, judicial, and quasi-judicial functions
in the municipal, provincial, and federal spheres of Canadian
government. Refereed by academics and practitioners; 2-3 months
for editorial decision; 3-6 months to publish; 27% accepted for
publication.

215. *Community Development Journal.* 1966. 3. Index.
      B. K. Taylor. Social Administration, The New University
      of Ulster, Coleraine, N. Ireland, United Kingdom.

      This is a scholarly journal for academics and practi-
tioners involved with community development. It publishes
articles dealing with community development problems, politics,
planning, programs, participation, and action world-wide, but
with special reference to the Third World. Refereed by academics and practitioners; 6 months for editorial decision; 6-
12 months to publish; 20% accepted for publication.

216. *Development and Change.* 1969. 4. Index. Martin
      Doornbos, Raymond Apthorpe, Kurt Martin. Institute of
      Social Studies, Badhuisweg 251, 2597 JR, The Hague,
      Netherlands.

      This interdisciplinary journal is for scholars and
practitioners who are concerned with the problems of developing countries. Its subject fields include rural development,
regional planning, bureaucracies, technology transfer, the role
of multinationals, educational and manpower policies, with an
emphasis on empirically based articles. Refereed by academics;
2 months for editorial decision; 6 months to publish; 10%
accepted for publication.

217. *Economic and Social Review.* 1969. 4. Index. Cum. Ind.
      Peter Mooney, Patrick Geary, and David Rottman.
      Economic and Social Studies, 4 Burlington Road, Dublin
      4, Ireland.

      This quarterly review publishes papers on all aspects of
the social sciences that are of general interest, with a partic-

ular focus on Ireland. Its subject fields include economics, sociology, demography, politics, social geography, psychology, and statistics. Refereed by academics and practitioners; 6-9 months for editorial decision; 3 months to publish; 50% accepted for publication.

218. *Human Relations*. 1947. 12. Index. Michael Foster, Tavistock Center, 120 Belsize Lane, London NW3 5BA, England.

This journal is founded on the belief that social scientists in all fields should work toward an integration of their attempts to understand the complexities of human problems. Many of the articles deal with organizational and managerial behavior that seeks to link theory with practice. Manuscripts are encouraged from those studying human problems within and between disciplines. Editorial information not available.

219. *Indian Journal of Public Administration*. 1955. 4. Index. Cum. Ind. J. N. Chaturvedi. Indian Institute of Public Administration, Indraprastha Estate, Ring Road, New Delhi 110002, India.

This journal, with international subscribers, reports on activities of the Indian Institute of Public Administration, and presents information, discussion and reviews of topics in public administration, law, constitutions, comparative administrative structures and functions, and administration of economic and social policies. Refereed by academics and practitioners; 3 months for editorial decision; 6 months to publish; 33% accepted for publication.

220. *International Development Review*. 1958. 4. Index. Andrew E. Rice. Society for International Development, Palazzo Civiltà del Lavoro, 00144 Rome, Italy.

This multidisciplinary journal, for persons involved with national or international development programs, covers economic, social and cultural aspects of development with particular attention to North-South affairs and alternative development strategies and lifestyles. Editor decides; 1-1½ months for editorial decision; 2-3 months to publish; 30% accepted for publication.

221. *International Organization*. 1947. 4. Peter J. Katzenstein. Cornell University, Ithaca, New York 14853.

This quarterly journal of the World Peace Foundation is intended for "people with a sophisticated scholarly understanding of international relations." It features scholarly articles on comparative foreign policy, international political economy,

and other issues of world politics, in addition to its traditional emphasis on international institutions. Refereed by
academics and practitioners; 1½-2 months for editorial decision;
4 months to publish; 10-15% accepted for publication.

222. *Journal of Conflict Resolution.* 1957. 4. Index.
      Bruce Russett. P. O. Box 3532, New Haven, Connecticut
      06520.

This scholarly journal publishes multidisciplinary empirical and theoretical papers on conflict between and within
nations. Contributions are drawn primarily from the fields of
psychology and political science, with some attention to economics and business management. Refereed by academics; 3 months
for editorial decision; 4-8 months to publish; 20% accepted for
publication.

223. *Journal of Developing Areas.* 1966. 4. Index.
      Nicholas C. Pano. Western Illinois University, Macomb,
      Illinois 61455.

This multidisciplinary journal, with a focus on the Third
World, lesser developed regions of developed countries, and the
development process, is intended for practitioners in business,
government and non-government organizations, as well as for the
academic community. Refereed by academics and practitioners;
2-4 months for editorial decision; 12-15 months to publish;
10-12% accepted for publication.

224. *Journal of Development Studies.* 1964. 4. Index.
      Cum. Ind. Michael Lipton. 11 Gainsborough Road, London
      E11 1RS, England.

This quarterly journal is for the academic community and
professionals in the field of economic and social development.
It features a broad range of articles and commentaries devoted
to the social, economic, and political aspects of development.
Refereed by academics; 3 months for editorial decision; 3-6
months to publish; % accepted not available.

225. *Management.* 1953. 12. Index. Cum. Ind. Alex Miller.
      Irish Management Institute, Sandyford Road, Dublin 14,
      Ireland.

This is a monthly business journal for senior and middle
managers focusing on management practice and management developments. Articles relate to the general and functional areas
of management, behavioral science, and politico-economic issues.
Editor decides; 3 weeks for editorial decision; 2-3 months to
publish; 50% accepted for publication.

226. *Management International Review.* 1959. 4. Index.
K. Macharzina. Universitat Hohenheim (09100), Schloss-
Postfach 106, D-7000 Stuttgart 70, Federal Republic of
Germany.

Sponsored by the European Foundation for Management
Development, this is a quarterly English language journal which
seeks to promote international comparative study in management
and international business. Its subject fields include international business, trans-national corporations, comparative
management, and management development. Refereed by academics
and practitioners; 3-4 months for editorial decision; 2 months
to publish; 50% accepted for publication.

227. *National Development/Modern Government.* 1954. 9.
Martin Greenburgh. P. O. Box 5017, Westport, Connecticut 06880.

A professional journal in magazine format, this periodical is circulated to government officials and technical experts
in Africa, Asia, the Middle East, and Latin America. It publishes articles carrying technical and practical information on
the development of national infrastructures, government operations, and national planning in the Third World. Editor decides
and occasionally refereed; 1 week for editorial decision; 4
months to publish; 20% accepted for publication.

228. *Orbis: A Journal of World Affairs.* 1955. 4. Index.
William R. Kintner. Foreign Policy Research Institute,
3508 Market Street, Philadelphia, Pennsylvania 19104.

Published by the Foreign Policy Research Institute,
this quarterly journal covers all aspects of world affairs and
foreign policy, with emphasis on security relations, political
issues, and economic problems for an audience of scholars,
government officials, and the interested public. Refereed by
academics; 2 weeks-2 months for editorial decision; 3 months
to publish; 5% accepted for publication.

229. *Philippine Journal of Public Administration.* 1957. 4.
Index. Dr. Ledivina V. Carino. College of Public Admin-
istration, University of the Philippines, P. O. Box 74,
Manila, Philippines.

This quarterly journal, for academics, practitioners and
students, both in the Philippines and internationally, publishes
articles on developments in Philippine public administration
and the practice of public administration internationally.
Editor decides; 1-2 months for editorial decision; 3-4 months
to publish; 50% accepted for publication.

230. *Planning and Administration.* 1974. 2. Cum. Ind.
      E. M. Harloff. Wassenaarseweg 45 2596GC, The Hague,
      Netherlands.

      Planning and Administration is published jointly by
the International Union of Local Authorities (IULA) and the
International Federation for Housing and Planning. It publishes
case studies and articles of a general nature on all facets of
local government and public administration, for an audience of
local government practitioners and the academic community.
Editor and selected advisors decide; 1 month for editorial
decision; 4-6 months to publish; 75% accepted for publication.

231. *Public Administration.* 1923. 4. Index. J. M. Lee.
      Department of Politics, University of Bristol, Bristol
      B58 1US, England.

      Public Administration contains articles focusing on
analysis and discussion of administrative problems and experience, with emphasis on British public administration. Its
articles are predominantly non-technical and include historical studies. Editor and associate editor decide; 3-4 months
for editorial decision; 1 year to publish; 25-35% accepted for
publication.

232. *Public Administration and Development.* 1981. 4. Index.
      David J. Murray. Royal Institute of Public Administration,
      Hamilton House, Mabledon Place, London WC1H 9BD, England.

      Sponsored by the Royal Institute, this new quarterly jour-
nal "reviews and assesses experiments and experience in the practice of public administration where this is directed to developmen
in Third World countries." PAD continues the work of the former
Journal of Administration Overseas and sustains the distinctive
contribution of its predecessor with its emphasis on the considera
tion of administrative practice at local, regional and national
levels. It gives special attention to features of public administration and development which have an interest and importance beyond a particular government and state, for instance, the growing
importance of public administration in public corporations and
economic enterprise, and in para-statal organizations. Refereed
by academics and practitioners; 2-3 months for editorial decision;
5-8 months to publish; 25% accepted for publication.

233. *Public Sector.* 1978. 4. Index. Cum. Ind. S. Arnold
      and R. Gregory. New Zealand Institute of Public Adminis-
      tration, Box 5032, Wellington, New Zealand.

      A practitioner-oriented journal, *Public Sector* focuses
on public administration and policy-making in both central and
local government. It publishes topical, often controversial
articles, striving for high reader impact. Refereed by New
Zealand Institute; 1 month for editorial decision; 6 months
to publish; 75% accepted for publication.

234. *Quarterly Journal of Administration.* 1966. 4. Index.
     Cum. Ind. R. I. Onwuka. Faculty of Administration,
     University of Ife, Ile-Ife, Nigeria.

     This quarterly journal, for academics and practitioners,
is devoted to the dissemination of research and exchange of
knowledge relating to all aspects of public administration and
international affairs. Refereed by academics and practitioners;
1-3 months for editorial decision; 1 year to publish; 40-50%
accepted for publication.

235. *Social and Economic Studies.* 1953. 4. Index. Cum. Ind.
     Vaughan Lewis. Institute of Social and Economic Research,
     University of the West Indies, Mona, Kingston 7, Jamaica.

     This quarterly journal, for academics and professionals,
is devoted to the social, economic and political problems of the
Caribbean and other developing areas and countries. It publishes
both theoretical and empirical studies on a broad range of topics
in social and economic development. Refereed by academics and
practitoners; 6 months for editorial decision; 8 months to publish; 25% accepted for publication.

236. *Studies in Comparative International Development.* 1964.
     4. Index forthcoming. Jay Weinstein. Department of
     Social Sciences, Georgia Institute of Technology,
     Atlanta, Georgia 30332.

     This is a journal of interdisciplinary research and
policy analysis focusing on the development process, including
economic and political development, social change, technology
transfer and innovation, population growth and migration, and
general development theory. Refereed by academics and practitioners; 6 months for editorial decision; 6 months to publish;
15% accepted for publication.

237. *Sudan Journal of Administration and Development.* 1965.
     1. Osman Kheiri. Institute of Public Administration,
     P. O. Box 1492, Khartoum, Sudan.

     The focus of this journal is public administration and
socio-economic development. Its primary concern is with problems of administrative reform within the context of the socio-
economic development of the Sudan. It also provides a forum
for world-wide experience, especially Afro-Arab, in the field of
development. Refereed by academics and practitioners; 2 months
for editorial decision; 3 months to publish; 80% accepted for
publication.

238. *World Affairs*. 1928. 4. Index. Cornelius W. Vahle,
     Jr. The American Peace Society, 4000 Albemarle Street,
     N. W., Room 402, Washington, D. C. 20016.

     This quarterly presents articles that explore the issues
involved in international conflict. Its topic areas include
international relations, law and organization; foreign policy;
comparative politics; and diplomatic history. Refereed by
academics; 2 months for editorial decision; 4 months to publish;
40% accepted for publication.

239. *World Politics*. 1948. 4. Index. Elsbeth G. Lewin.
     112 Corwin Hall, Princeton University, Princeton, New
     Jersey 08540.

     This is a multi-disciplinary scholarly journal concerned
with problems of international relations and national development. Subject fields include comparative and international
politics, foreign policy, and international relations theory.
Refereed by academics; 2-4 months for editorial decision; 6-
12 months to publish; 12% accepted for publication.

VI. EDUCATION ADMINISTRATION

240. *Educational Administration*. 1971. 3. Cum. Ind.
     Ray Bolam. Coombe Lodge - F. E. Staff College, Blagdon,
     Bristol BS18 6RG, England.

     Sponsored by the British Education Administration
Society, the purpose of this journal is to "provide a forum
between academics and practitioners across all levels of educational administration." Refereed by academics and practitioners; 1 month for editorial decision; 3 months to publish;
40% accepted for publication.

241. *Educational Administration Quarterly*. 1964. 3. Index.
     Daniel E. Griffiths. SEHNAP, New York University, Press
     Building 42, New York, New York 10003.

     This publication provides a forum for discourse among
educational administration scholars, practicing administrators,
social and behavioral scientists, and others concerned with the
expansion of knowledge basic to an improved understanding of
administrative behavior in complex educational organizations.
Refereed by academics; 1½-2 months for editorial decision; 6-9
months to publish; 10% accepted for publication.

242. *Educational Evaluation and Policy Analysis.* 1979. 6.
Index. James Popham. American Educational Research
Association, 1230 17th Street, N. W., Washington, D. C.
20036.

This bi-monthly journal focuses on educational evaluation,
educational policy analysis, and the relationship between the
two activities, dealing not only with the theoretical and
methodological issues, but also with the practical concerns
of individuals engaged in the evaluation enterprises and the
formulation of educational policy. Refereed by academics and
practitioners; 3 months for editorial decision; 3-6 months to
publish; 30% accepted for publication.

243. *Journal of Educational Administration.* 1963. 2.
A. Ross Thomas. Centre for Administrative Studies,
University of New England, Armidale, N. S. W. 2351,
Australia.

This quarterly journal covers all aspects of educational
administration at elementary and higher education levels for
scholars, educators, and others interested in the study and practice of educational administration. Refereed by academics and
practitioners; 2 months for editorial decision; 1 year to publish; 20-25% accepted for publication.

244. *Journal of Higher Education.* 1930. 6. Index.
Robert J. Silverman. Ohio State University Press,
316 Hitchcock Hall, 2070 Neil Avenue, Columbus, Ohio
43210.

Affiliated with the American Association for Higher
Education, this bi-monthly publication deals with all aspects
of higher education and is intended for academic and non-
academic administrators and faculty in all fields of study.
Refereed by academics and practitioners; $\frac{1}{2}$-2$\frac{1}{2}$ months for editorial decision; 6 months to 1 year to publish; 8% accepted
for publication.

245. *Planning and Changing.* 1970. 4. Mary Ann Lynn.
Department of Education Administration and Foundations,
Illinois State University, Normal, Illinois 61761.

A quarterly journal for educational administrators and
scholars, *Planning and Changing* reports the processes and
effects of planning and changing upon educational systems. Its
articles are oriented toward education research and theory, and
program practice and change, with an emphasis on planning systems
and administrative tasks. Refereed by academics; 1$\frac{1}{2}$ months for

editorial decision; 1½-3 months to publish; 50% accepted for publication.

VII. ENVIRONMENTAL MANAGEMENT

246. *Computers, Environment and Urban Systems.* 1975. 4.
      Index. Cum. Ind. Gordon Gebert. City College, School
      of Architecture and Environmental Studies, 138th Street
      and Convent Avenue, New York, New York 10013.

      This international journal disseminates information,
theory and opinion regarding the computer's role in understanding, controlling and planning human activities which affect the
environment, both natural and man-made. The journal's subject
fields include computers, the environment, planning, urban
studies and policy-making; the intended audience is the academic
community, professionals, policy analysts and policy-makers,
and the informed public. It is published in cooperation with
the Urban and Regional Information Systems Association. Refereed by academics and practitioners; 3 months for editorial
decision; 3 months to publish; 70% accepted for publication.

247. *CONTACT - Journal of Urban and Environmental Affairs.*
      1975. 3. R. F. Keith. Faculty of Environmental
      Studies, University of Waterloo, Waterloo, Ontario
      N2L 3G1, Canada.

      CONTACT provides analyses of urban and environmental
issues, with emphasis on policy aspects and conceptual, theoretical and methodological advances; it is intended for policy-
makers, environmental and planning practitioners and the academic community. Refereed by academics and practitioners; 2
months for editorial decision; 1 year to publish; % accepted
not available.

248. *EKISTICS.* 1957. 10. Index. P. Psomopoulos.
      Athens Center of Ekistics, P. O. Box 471, Athens,
      Greece.

      The subject field of this journal is "Ekistics," the
problems and science of human settlements. Each issue is devoted to one topic concerning human settlements such as housing, planning, communication, education, energy, and environment. The intended audience includes academics and students
of all disciplines, practitioners and public officials, and
the general public. Editors decide; 6 months for editorial
decision; 3-6 months to publish; 50% accepted for publication.

249. *Journal of Environmental Management*. 1973. 6.
J. N. R. Jeffers. Institute of Terrestial Ecology,
Merlewood Research Station, Grange-over-Sands, Cumbria,
LA11 6JU, England.

This bi-monthly journal, for the scientific community,
resource managers, planners, and administrators, publishes
technical and non-technical papers "devoted to the management
of the environment toward desired aims." Refereed by academics
and practitioners; 4 months for editorial decision; 8-10 months
to publish; 70% accepted for publication.

250. *Technological Forecasting and Social Change*. 1969. 12.
Index. Cum. Ind. Dr. Harold A. Linstone. Futures Research Institute, Portland State University, P. O. Box
751, Portland, Oregon 97207.

This is an international journal devoted to the methodology and practice of technology forecasting and assessment, and
the interaction of technology with the social, behavioral and
environmental aspects of integrative planning. Its audience
includes industry and government planners and the academic community. Refereed by academics and practitioners; 1-2 months
for editorial decision; 6-12 months to publish; 40% accepted
for publication.

251. *Traffic Quarterly*. 1947. 4. Index. Cum. Ind.
Robert S. Holmes. Box 55, Saugatuck Station, Westport,
Connecticut 06880.

Sponsored by the Eno Foundation for Transportation,
Traffic Quarterly presents articles on a broad range of subjects relevant to transportation. Intended for an audience of
transportation administrators, planners, consultants and students, the journal's subject fields include all modes of transportation of people and goods, concentrating on planning, administration, finance, socioeconomic and environmental factors,
and functional design. Refereed by academics and practitioners;
3-6 weeks for editorial decision; 1-5 months to publish; 12-15%
accepted for publication.

252. *Transportation*. 1971. 4. David T. Hartgen. Basic
Research Unit, New York State Department of Transportation, 1220 Washington Avenue, Albany, New York 12226.

Transportation is an international journal of transportation analysis, design and planning. Interaction between transportation activities and the social, economic and environmental
aspects of urban life are given particular attention, with

emphasis on the systems approach. Refereed by academics and
practitioners; time for editorial decision not stated; 3-5
months to publish; 30-40% accepted for publication.

253. *Transportation Research.* (Part A: General, Part B:
     Methodological). Part A: Bi-monthly, Part B: Quarterly.
     Index. Frank A. Haight. Research Building B, University
     Park, Pennsylvania 16802.

Transportation Research publishes scientific and technical articles dealing with the design and operation of transportation systems, including economic factors such as pricing,
cost effectiveness, and criteria for modal comparison, along
with more general issues of transportation policy and planning.
Refereed by academics and practitioners; 4 months for editorial
decision; 1 year to publish; 35% accepted for publication.

VIII. JUSTICE/LAW ENFORCEMENT

254. *Crime and Delinquency.* 1955. 4. Index. Sarah T. Dike.
     National Council on Crime and Delinquency, 411 Hackensack
     Avenue, Hackensack, New Jersey 07601.

This quarterly journal is a publication of the National
Council on Crime and Delinquency. Its audience includes the
academic community, practitioners, and others interested in the
study of the criminal justice system. The journal publishes
original research on crime and delinquency; new theory; critical
analysis of the state of criminal justice in the United States,
and occasionally abroad; and descriptive essays and commentaries
on the administration of criminal and juvenile justice. Editor
decides; 1½ months for editorial decision; 18 months to publish;
10-15% accepted for publication.

255. *Criminal Justice and Behavior.* 1974. 4. Index.
     Dan M. Gottredson. Sage Publications, Inc., 275 South
     Beverly Drive, Beverly Hills, California 90212.

Sponsored by the American Association of Correctional
Psychologists, this scholarly journal is devoted to scientific
and professional perspectives from the behavioral sciences on
problems of crime, delinquency, corrections, and justice.
Refereed by academics and practitioners; 2 months for editorial
decision; 8 months to publish; 25% accepted for publication.

256. *Criminology: An Interdisciplinary Journal.* 1963. 4.
     James A. Inciardi. Division of Criminal Justice, Univ-
     ersity of Delaware, Newark, Delaware 19711.

Criminology is the official journal of the American
Society of Criminology. It is an interdisciplinary journal devoted to the study of crime and deviant behavior, as found in
the disciplines of law, criminal justice, and the social and
behavioral sciences. Articles focus on original research,
behavioral and historical issues, reviews and discussions of
current issues, and controversies in the area of crime and
justice. Refereed by academics and practitioners; 3 months
for editorial decision; 8-12 months to publish; 14% accepted
for publication.

257. *Federal Probation*. 1937. 4. Index. Cum. Ind.
      Donald L. Chamlee. Administrative Office of the United
      States Courts, Washington, D. C. 20544.

This publication, for persons who work with offenders,
for criminal justice scholars, and the informed public, covers
the broad area of crime and delinquency treatment and prevention. Its subject fields include criminology, penology, sociology, psychology, and psychiatry. Editor decides; 1 month for
editorial decision; 6 months to publish; 20% accepted for publication.

258. *Journal of Criminal Law and Criminology*. 1910. 4.
      Index. Cum. Ind. Bobbie C. McGee. 357 E. Chicago
      Avenue, Chicago, Illinois 60611.

This scholarly journal publishes articles in all areas
of criminal law and criminology for academics, jurists, legislators, and practitioners. Refereed by academics; 2 weeks
criminal law, 2½ months criminology for editorial decision; 3
months to publish; 18% accepted for publication.

259. *Journal of Police Science and Administration*. 1973.
      4. Index. Fred E. Inbau. International Association
      of Chiefs of Police, 11 Firstfield Road, Gaithersburg,
      Maryland 26760.

This publication includes articles, case studies, research projects and technical data on police science and administration topics for academics, police, and practitioners in the
criminal justice field. Refereed by academics and practitioners;
1½ months for editorial decision; 6-8 months to be published;
40-50% accepted for publication.

260. *Justice System Journal*. 1974. 3. Index.
      Russell Wheeler. The Institute for Court Management,
      1624 Market Street, Denver, Colorado 80202.

Sponsored by the Institute for Court Management, this
is a quarterly journal for academics and practitioners interested in how the courts operate and how they are managed. It

reports research and experience in the field of court management,
judicial administration, and related justice system areas.
Refereed by academics and practitioners; 1-2 months for editorial decision; 6-12 months for publication; 30% accepted for
publication.

IX.   ORGANIZATION THEORY AND BEHAVIOR

261.   *Exchange: The Organizational Behavior Teaching Journal.*
       1975. 4. Index. David L. Bradford. The Organization-
       al Behavior Teaching Society. School of Business Admin-
       istration, Box U-41 BR, The University of Connecticut,
       Storrs, Connecticut 06268.

This journal, for scholars and students of organizational
behavior and theory, and for training program staff in public
and private organizations, publishes conceptual and empirical
articles on the theory and technique of teaching organizational
behavior. Articles range from major conceptual pieces about
what is (and should be) taught to descriptions of specific
exercises and teaching techniques. Refereed by academics; 1½
months for editorial decision; 5 months to publish; 33% accepted for publication.

262.   *Group and Organizational Studies.* 1976. 4. Index.
       John E. Jones and Marshall Sashkin. University Associ-
       ates, Inc., 8517 Production Avenue, P. O. Box 26240,
       San Diego, California 92126.

This international journal, written for group facili-
tators, educators, and consultants in human relations training,
contains practice-oriented articles on leadership and management
development, personal growth, intercultural communication,
couples consultation, and organization and community development. Refereed by academics and practitioners; 2½ months for
editorial decision; 2½ months to publish; 25% accepted for
publication.

263.   *Human Communication Research.* 1974. 4. Mark L. Knapp.
       Purdue University, Department of Communication, West
       Lafayette, Indiana 47907.

This interdisciplinary journal, sponsored by the International Communication Association, publishes data-based articles
and literature reviews on information systems and human communi-
cation--interpersonal, mass, organizational, instructional,
political, health, and cross-cultural. Refereed by academics;
3-4 months for editorial decision; 3-4 months for publishing;
18% accepted for publication.

264. *Human Organization*. 1941. 4. Index. H. Russell Bernard.
     Department of Anthropology, University of Florida, Gaines-
     ville, Florida 32611.

   The official journal of the Society for Applied Anthropology, *Human Organization* publishes articles for applied
social scientists in the area of anthropology, sociology,
management, and public health. Refereed by academics; 2 months
for editorial decision; 6-12 months to publish; 15% accepted
for publication.

265. *International Studies of Management and Organization*.
     1971. 4. J. J. Boddewyn. Baruch College, 17 Lexington
     Avenue, New York, New York 10010.

   This quarterly journal publishes translations and reproductions of articles and proceedings originally published outside the United States in the fields of organization theory,
administrative science, and management practice. Refereed by
academics; 1-12 months for editorial decision; 3-12 months to
publish; 50% accepted for publication.

266. *Journal of Applied Psychology*. 1911. 6. Index.
     John P. Campbell. 1200 Seventeenth Street, N. W.
     Washington, D. C. 20036.

   A publication of the American Psychological Association,
this scholarly journal is devoted primarily to original investi-
gations that contribute new knowledge and understanding to any
field of applied psychology, except clinical psychology. Refereed by academics and practitioners; 2 weeks for editorial decision; 4-6 months for publishing; 20% accepted for publication.

267. *Journal of Humanistic Psychology*. 1961. 4. Index.
     Cum. Ind. Thomas C. Greening. Association for Human-
     istic Psychology, 325 Ninth Street, San Francisco,
     California 94103.

   This interdisciplinary journal publishes articles on
a broad range of topics such as authenticity, encounter, con-
sciousness, self-actualization, self-transcendence, creativity,
personal growth, holistic healing, confluent education, values,
and identity. Refereed by academics and practitioners; 1
week-3 months for editorial decision; 12 months to publish;
10% accepted for publication.

268. *Journal of Personality and Social Psychology*. 1932.
     12. Index. Ivan D. Steiner. Department of Psychology,
     University of Massachusetts, Amherst, Massachusetts
     01002.

This is a monthly publication of the American Psychological Association. The *Journal* publishes papers in all areas of personality and social psychology, emphasizing empirical studies but also including specialized theoretical, methodological, and review papers. Articles focus on a variety of topics, including attitudes and social cognition, interpersonal relations and group processes, personality processes and individual differences. Refereed by academics and practitioners; 2 months for editorial decision; 8 months to publish; 20% accepted for publication.

269. *Journal of Social Psychology.* 1929. 6. Leonard W. Doob. The Journal Press, 2 Commercial Street, Box 543, Provincetown, Massachusetts 02657.

This is a journal primarily for research-oriented psychologists. It focuses on studies of persons in group settings and on research dealing with culture and personality, with special attention to cross-cultural articles, field research, and briefly reported replications and refinements. Refereed by academics and practitioners; 1 month for editorial decision; 12 months to publish; 50% accepted for publication.

270. *Journal of Value Inquiry.* 1967. 4. Index. James B. Wilbur. Department of Philosophy, State University College, Geneseo, New York 14454.

This scholarly journal is devoted to questions concerning the nature, origin, experience and scope of value in general, as well as more restricted studies in problems of value in ethics, social and legal theory and practice. Editors decide; 3 months for editorial decision; 6-12 months to publish; 15% accepted for publication.

271. *Organizational Dynamics.* 1972. 4. Index. Dr. W. Warner Burke. AMACOM, 135 West 50th Street, New York, New York 10020.

A publication of the American Management Association, *Organizational Dynamics* is a quarterly review of organizational behavior for professional managers and scholars. Issues typically consist of essays and reviews of a range of topics in organization behavior, including management of people, leadership, organizational change, and human resource management. Refereed by academics and practitioners; 2-3 months for editorial decision; 6-9 months to publish; 20% accepted for publication.

272. *Organization Studies*. 1980. 4. David J. Hickson.
University of Bradford Management Centre, EMM Lane,
Bradford BD9 4JL, West Yorkshire, England.

Sponsored by the European Group for Organization
Studies, this quarterly journal includes theoretical and empirical papers on organizations and their members with emphasis
on the societal context of organizations and on societal differences. Topic areas include organization theory, sociology
of organizations, and cross-national comparison. Refereed by
academics; 3 months for editorial decision; 6 months to publish; 30% accepted for publication.

273. *Small Group Behavior*. 1970. 4. Index. Fred Massarik.
4320 Cedarhurst Circle, Los Angeles, California 90027.

This is a quarterly journal devoted to research, theory
and practice relating to small groups in counseling, T-groups,
laboratory and encounter groups; and psychotherapy. It publishes empirical, experimental, clinical, and theoretically
oriented articles drawing upon the fields of social and clinical psychology, sociology, and applied social science. Refereed by academics and practitioners; 3 months for editorial
decision; 6-9 months to publish; 10-15% accepted for publication.

X. PUBLIC FINANCE

274. *Journal of Financial and Quantitative Analysis*. 1965.
5. Index. Cum. Ind. Robert C. Higgins. Graduate
School of Business, University of Washington, Seattle,
Washington 98195.

Published in cooperation with the Western Finance
Association, this scholarly journal for scholars and practitioners in finance and economics, specializes in research articles
on corporation finance, securities, markets, and related areas.
Refereed by academics; 3 months for editorial decision; 8
months to publish; 20% accepted for publication.

275. *Journal of Law and Economics*. 1958. 2. Cum. Ind.
R. H. Coase and William M. Landers. The University of
Chicago Law School, 111 East 60th Street, Chicago,
Illinois 60637.

Primarily for lawyers and economists, this journal publishes articles in the fields of law and economics, with special
emphasis on topics such as antitrust and regulation. Refereed
by academics; 6-10 weeks for editorial decision; 1 year to publish; 10% accepted for publication.

276. *Journal of Public Economics*. 1972. 6. Index.
     Cum. Ind. A. B. Atkinson. London School of Economics,
     Houghton Street, London WC2A 2AE, England.

This bi-monthly publication, for academic researchers
and professionals concerned with public policy in government
and industry, aims to "encourage original scientific contributions to the problem of public sector economics," with particular emphasis given to the application of modern economic
theory and methods of quantitative analysis. Refereed by academics; 3-6 months for editorial decision; 2-3 months to publish; 15% accepted for publication.

277. *Public Finance*. 1946. 3. Index. Professor
     Dieter Biehl. Technische Universitat, Berun-West,
     Uhlandstr., 4-5, D--1000 Berlin 12, West Germany.

This international journal of public finance studies,
intended for academics, the business community, and those working in government financial institutions, publishes articles on
the theoretical and empirical aspects of public finance and related issues. Refereed by academics and practitioners; time
varies for editorial decision; 3 months to publish; % accepted
not available.

278. *Public Finance and Accountancy*. 1974. 12. Index.
     Philip Windsor. The Chartered Institute of Public
     Finance and Accountancy, 1 Buckingham Palace, London
     SWE 6HS, England.

PFA is the official journal of one of the major accountancy bodies in the U. K. (CIPFA), specializing in the public
sector. The journal is aimed toward an audience of public
sector financial managers and accountants. It publishes articles relating to accounting, auditing, and financial management
in the public sector. Refereed by academics and practitioners;
4-6 weeks for editorial decision; 8-10 weeks to publish; 10%
accepted for publication.

XI. PUBLIC PERSONNEL ADMINISTRATION

279. *Industrial Relations*. 1961. 3. Index. David S. Bowen.
     Institute of Industrial Relations, University of Cali-
     fornia, Berkeley, California 94720.

Industrial Relations, for academics, labor and management professionals, publishes articles on all aspects of the
employment relationship such as labor economics, sociology,
psychology, political science and law. Refereed by academics;

1-2 months for editorial decision; 2-6 months to publish; 10%
accepted for publication.

280. *Industrial Society.* 1918. 4. Index. Chloe Mailer.
    3 Carlton House Terrace, London SW1Y 5DG, England.

    This publication covers management-industrial relations
for line managers of every level, and gives examples of good
organizational practices in the United Kingdom and overseas.

281. *International Labour Review.* 1921. 6. Index.
    David Hobden. International Labour Office, CH 1211,
    Geneva 22, Switzerland.

    This bi-monthly ILO publication is aimed at a broad
audience of academics, government officials, and employer and
worker organizations. The *Review* seeks to contribute to a
wider understanding of questions of labor and social policy
and administration through the results of original research,
international comparative studies, and analyses of international experiences in the areas of labor economics, education and
training, social security, collective bargaining, income promotion, labor-management relations, and national and international legislation. The chief editor, advised by experts from
the ILO, decides; 2 months for editorial decision; 6-10 months
to publish; 10% accepted for publication.

282. *Journal of Employment Counseling.* 1963. 4. Cum. Ind.
    David P. Meyer. American Personnel and Guidance Asso-
    ciation, Two Skyline Place, 5203 Leesburg Pike, Falls
    Church, Virginia 22041.

    This official publication of the National Employment
Counselors Association covers issues such as employment counseling, occupational information, counselor education and
training, career development, and employment/training policy
for practitioners and other interested professionals, through
reporting of professional experimentation or research in these
areas. Refereed by academics and practitioners; 2 months for
editorial decision; 1 year to publish; 50% accepted for publication.

283. *Journal of Human Resources.* 1966. 4. Index.
    Stanley H. Masters. Social Science Building, University
    of Wisconsin, Madison, Wisconsin 53706.

    The subject fields for this scholarly journal are labor
economics and the economics of health, welfare, and education.
It features empirical studies analyzing the role of education

and training in enhancing production skills, employment opportunities, and income, as well as of manpower, health, and welfare policies as they relate to the labor market and to economic and social development. Refereed by academics; 3 months for editorial decision; time to publish not stated; 10-12% accepted for publication.

284. *Journal of Personality.* 1932. 4. Index. Philip R. Costanzo. Department of Psychology, Duke University, Durham, North Carolina 27706.

The *Journal of Personality* is devoted to scientific inquiry in the field of personality. It publishes empirical articles on personality structure, function, and development; personality and social processes; and behavior dynamics. Refereed by academics and practitioners; 4 months for editorial decision; 8-12 months to publish; 15% accepted for publication.

285. *Journal of Vocational Behavior.* 1971. 6. Index. Lenore W. Harmon. 210 Education, University of Illinois, Urbana, Illinois 61801.

This journal publishes empirical, methodological, and theoretical articles related to such issues as the validation of theoretical constructs, developments in instrumentation, program comparisons, and research methodology as related to vocational development, preference, choice and selection, implementation, satisfaction and effectiveness. Refereed by academics; 2-3 months for editorial decision; 1 year to publish; 35% accepted for publication.

286. *Monthly Labor Review.* 1915. 12. Index. Henry Lowenstern. Bureau of Labor Statistics, Room 2029 GAO Building, 441 G Street N. W., Washington, D. C. 20212.

The *Review* publishes the results of the Bureau of Labor Statistics' major studies and statistical series, as well as manuscripts on labor economics and related topics. Editors decide; 4-5 weeks for editorial decision; 6-8 weeks to publish; 20% accepted for publication.

287. *Personnel Administrator.* 1955. 12. Index. Margaret McClure Nemec. 30 Park Drive, Berea, Ohio 44017.

Personnel Administrator is a publication of the American Society for Personnel Administration. It covers a broad range of topic areas, seeking to provide personnel and industrial relations practitioners and students in the field with new concepts in human resources management, industrial relations, and personnel management. Refereed by academics and practi-

tioners; 1½ months for editorial decision; 1-12 months to publish; 50% accepted for publication.

288. *Personnel and Guidance Journal.* 1921. 10. Index.
      Cum. Ind. James Barclay. American Personnel and
      Guidance Association, Two Skyline Place, Suite 400,
      5203 Leesburg Pike, Falls Church, Virginia 22041.

This practitioner-oriented journal publishes articles
that deal with current professional and scientific issues in
personnel and guidance, new techniques or innovative practices
and programs, critical integrations of published research,
and research reports of significance to practitioners. Refereed by academics and practitioners; 3 months for editorial decision; 6 months to publish; 20% accepted for publication.

289. *Personnel Journal.* 1922. 12. Index. Cum. Ind.
      Margaret Mangus. P. O. Box 2440, Costa Mesa, Cali-
      fornia 92626.

Personnel Journal's purpose is to "provide a source of
contemporary ideas, both theoretical and practical, for professionals in the personnel management and labor relations
field." Articles published cover a variety of topic areas, including personnel management, industrial relations, employee
relations, compensation and benefits, recruitment, and health
and safety. Editorial staff decides; 2 months for editorial
decision; 6 months to publish; 25% accepted for publication.

290. *Personnel Psychology.* 1947. 4. Index. Milton D.
      Haked. Department of Psychology, Ohio State University,
      Columbus, Ohio 43210.

Personnel Psychology is directed toward an audience of
personnel managers and psychologists. It publishes articles
on original research and critical reviews of the research literature in industrial and organizational psychology and administration of human resources. Refereed by academics and practitioners; 2-3 months for editorial decision; 3 months to publish; 30% accepted for publication.

291. *Relations Industrielle/Industrial Relations.* 1945. 4.
      Index. Cum. Ind. Gerard Dion. Departement de relations
      industrielles, Université Laval, Quebec P. Q. G1K 7P4,
      Canada.

This quarterly journal publishes articles on all aspects
of industrial and labor relations with a particular, but not
exclusive, emphasis on the Canadian. Its subject fields include
industrial relations, labor economics, trade unionism, personnel

management, labor law and labor history. Its intended audience is public administrators, labor leaders, researchers and academics. Refereed by academics; 3 months for editorial decision; 6-9 months to publish; 50% accepted for publication.

292. *Review of Public Personnel Administration*. 1980. 3. Charlie B. Tyer. Bureau of Governmental Research and Service, University of South Carolina, Columbia, South Carolina 29208.

The objective of this journal is to "further the understanding of public personnel policy and administration by encouraging scholarship in public personnel management and labor relations." The *Review* publishes studies which analyze the effects of specific personnel procedures or programs on the management function and studies which assess the impact of personnel management on the broader areas of public policy and administration. Refereed by academics and practitioners; 2 months for editorial decision; 3-5 months to publish; % accepted not available.

293. *Sociology of Work and Occupation*. 1973. 4. Marie Haug. Department of Sociology, Case Western Reserve University, Cleveland, Ohio 44106.

Intended for an audience of sociologists, industrial psychologists and administrators, this quarterly journal is international in scope and features empirically based articles on issues related to work and occupations. Refereed by academics; 3 months for editorial decision; 6-9 months to publish; 20% accepted for publication.

294. *Texas Personnel and Guidance Association Journal*. 1972. 2. Index. Margie Norman. Texas Personnel and Guidance Association, 316 W. 12th Street, Suite 402, Austin, Texas 78701.

This journal is for an intended audience of personnel workers and counselors. Its articles are directed to topics of interest to personnel workers and counselors in schools, colleges, and community and government agencies. Editor decides; 9 weeks for editorial decision; 6 months to 1 year to publish; 60-80% accepted for publication.

295. *Training and Development*. 1947. 12. Index. Michael H. Cook. P. O. Box 5307, Madison, Wisconsin 53705.

The official publication of the American Society for Training and Development, this monthly periodical focuses on current trends in the training and human resource development

profession. Articles cover such topics as training and education in the world of work; human resource development; organizational development; and audio-visual aids in training and
development. Editor decides; 1-1½ months for editorial decision; time to publication varies; 10% accepted for publication.

296. *The Vocational Guidance Quarterly.* 1952. 4. Index.
Edwin A. Whitfield. National Vocational Guidance
Association, 6401 Linda Vista Road, San Diego, Califor-
nia 92111.

This practitioner-oriented journal publishes articles
dealing with career guidance and development, career education
and decision-making, career measurement and testing, and the
world of work. Refereed by academics and practitioners; 3
months for editorial decision; 3 months to publish; 30% accepted for publication.

XII. PUBLIC POLICY AND REGULATION

297. *Canadian Public Policy.* 1975. 4. Index. John
Vanderkamp. University of Guelph, Room 039 - Arts
Building, Guelph, Ontario N1G 2W1, Canada.

This publication aims to stimulate research and discussion of public policy problems in Canada in all areas of
economic, social, and cultural life at all three levels of
government. The journal is directed at a wide readership,
publishing policy-relevant articles primarily of a non-
technical nature. Refereed by academics and practitioners;
2 months for editorial decision; 2½ months to be published;
22% accepted for publication.

298. *Comparative Strategy: An International Journal.* 1978.
4. Index. Richard B. Foster. 3 East 44th Street,
New York, New York 10017.

This quarterly journal, which deals with political
science and international affairs, examines the political,
military, and economic dimensions of strategic issues and is
intended for the academic, research, governmental and business
communities.

299. *Foreign Affairs.* 1922. 5. Index. Cum. Ind.
William P. Bundy, Doris E. Forest. 58 East 68th
Street, New York, New York 10021.

Sponsored by the Council on Foreign Relations, this
publication seeks to "inform public opinion by a broad

presentation of divergent ideas on world politics and international relations." Its special year-end issue, introduced
in 1978, focuses on "America and the World." Editorial staff
decides; 1-1½ months for editorial decision; 1-6 months to
publish; 5% accepted for publication.

300. *Foreign Policy.* 1970. 4. William Maynes. 11 Dupont
      Circle, N. W., Washington, D. C. 20036.

     Foreign Policy is a quarterly journal published by the
Carnegie Endowment for International Peace. Intended for a
broad audience of government officials, academics, and persons
involved or interested in foreign policy, the journal focuses
on American foreign policy and international relations. Editors
decide; 1-2 months for editorial decision; 1 month to publish;
10% accepted for publication.

301. *Journal of Communication.* 1950. 5. Index. George
      Gerbner. Annenberg School of Communications, University
      of Pennsylvania, Philadelphia, Pennsylvania 19104.

     This journal is concerned with the study of communica-
tion theory, practice, and policy, including fields such as
interpersonal communication, media research, telecommunications,
communications policy, and international communications. It is
intended for scholars, policy-makers, researchers, and professionals interested in research and policy developments and in
the impact and influence of communications. Academics and
practitioners referee; 6 months for editorial decision; 3
months to publish; 20% accepted for publication.

302. *Journal of Consumer Affairs.* 1967. 2. Monroe Friedman.
      Department of Psychology, Eastern Michigan University,
      Ypsilanti, Michigan 48197.

     An applied journal, with emphasis on consumer economics,
consumer education, and consumer protection policy, the *Journal
of Consumer Affairs* is intended for business executives, government consumer protection officials, and consumer educators.
Refereed by academics and practitioners; 4-5 months for editorial decision; 5-6 months to publish; 25% accepted for publication.

303. *Journal of Contemporary Studies.* 1978. 4. A. Laurence
      Chickering and Arnold Meltsner. Institute for Contempo-
      rary Studies, 260 California Street, San Francisco,
      California 94111.

     This general public policy quarterly emphasizes debate
on both foreign and domestic policy issues. It seeks to serve
as a platform for new policy ideas and in-depth analyses of

current programs. Editors decide; 4-6 weeks for editorial decision; 2-6 months to publish; 20% accepted for publication.

304. *Journal of Socio-Economic Planning Sciences.* 1964. 6.
     Index. Summer N. Levine. P. O. Box 116, Setauket,
     New York 11733.

     Socio-Economic Planning Sciences is devoted to the quan-
titative analysis of interdisciplinary problems in socio-economic
planning, particularly applications of systems analysis to the
planning of public welfare and community services. Topic areas
include analytical studies relating to the interaction of various
segments of society and technology; studies directed toward the
more effective utilization of public resources; and studies
devoted to the anticipation of future needs for social services.
Refereed by academics; 3 months for editorial decision; 5 months
to publish; % accepted not available.

305. *Law and Policy Quarterly.* 1979. 4. Index. Larry J.
     Cohen and John A. Gardiner. Department of Political
     Science, University of Illinois at Chicago Circle,
     Box 4348, Chicago, Illinois 60680.

     This quarterly journal publishes both theoretical and
empirical research articles dealing with the relationship between law and public policy, including critical analyses of the
legal process in general and of specific policy areas such as
criminal justice, health, housing, civil rights and so forth.
Its intended audience includes academics, researchers, and
professionals interested in law and policy issues. Refereed
by academics and practitioners; 2-2½ months for editorial
decision; 6 months to publish; 20% accepted for publication.

306. *Long Range Planning.* 1968. 6. Index. Bernard Taylor.
     The Administrative Staff College, Greenlands, Henley-
     on-Thames, Oxon, England.

     Long Range Planning is an international journal which
aims to "focus the attention of senior managers, administrators
and academics on the concepts and techniques involved in the
development and implementation of strategy and plans in business
and government. Refereed by academics and practitioners; 2
weeks for editorial decision; 6 months to publish; 85% accepted
for publication.

307. *Policy and Politics.* 1972. 4. Michael J. Hill.
     School for Advanced Urban Studies, University of Bristol,
     Rodney Lodge, Grange Road, Bristol, England.

This interdisciplinary journal has "an overall commit-
ment to the advancement of the policy process." It is intended
for those concerned with public policy-making and for those
studying the policy process, both in Britain and elsewhere.
Refereed by academics and practitioners; 1-1½ months for editorial decision; 3 months to publish; 50% accepted for publication.

308. *Policy Review.* 1977. 4. Index. John O'Sullivan.
     513 C Street, N. E., Washington, D. C. 20002.

Sponsored by the Heritage Foundation, this quarterly
journal publishes articles on a wide range of issues in both
foreign and domestic policy and is intended for government
officials, academics and the business community. Its subject
fields include economics, education, energy, government regulation, and foreign policy. Editor and editorial board decide;
1-4 months for editorial decision; 1-6 months to publish;
15% accepted for publication.

309. *Policy Sciences.* 1968. 4. Index. Peter de Leon.
     The Rand Corporation, 1700 Main Street, Santa Monica,
     California 90406.

Policy Sciences focuses on the study and improvement
of policy-making, providing a forum for papers that blend the
management disciplines--policy analysis, decision theory, and
similar analytic approaches--with the behavioral sciences.
It also pays special attention to normative requirements of
public policy and comparative policy analysis. Refereed by
academics and practitioners; 1½ months for editorial decision;
6-9 months to publish; 15% accepted for publication.

310. *Population and Development Review.* 1975. 4. Index.
     Cum. Ind. Paul Demeny. The Population Council,
     1 Dag Hammarskjold Plaza, New York, New York 10017.

Population and Development Review publishes studies
dealing with the interrelationships between population and
socioeconomic development and related issues of public policy.
It is intended for academics, policy-makers, and individuals
conducting applied research in demographics. Refereed by
academics; 2 months for editorial decision; 6 months to publish;
15-20% accepted for publication.

311. *Social Science Quarterly.* 1920. 4. Index. Charles
     M. Bonjean. The University of Texas at Austin, Austin,
     Texas 78712.

This scholarly journal publishes significant research findings, theoretical advances and new social science information of interest to scholars in more than a single social science discipline. *SSQ* articles focus on current social issues and traditional social science concerns; it also has a special concern for subjects with policy relevance. Refereed by academics and practitioners; 1-3 months for editorial decision; 4-7 months to publish; 11-13% accepted for publication.

312. *The World Today.* 1945. 12. Index. Liliana Brisby.
     Royal Institute of International Affairs, Chatham House,
     10 St. James Square, London SW1Y 4LE, England.

This journal serves a broad audience and publishes articles on international affairs, as well as political and economic analyses of individual countries or regions, written by authors with first-hand knowledge. Editor decides; 2 weeks-1 month for editorial decision; 1-6 months to publish; 30% accepted for publication.

XIII. SOCIAL SERVICES/HEALTH CARE ADMINISTRATION

313. *Administration in Mental Health.* 1974. 4. Index.
     Cum. Ind. Saul Feldman. P. O. Box 2088, Rockville,
     Maryland 20852.

A quarterly journal intended primarily for policy-makers *Administration in Mental Health* publishes conceptual and empirical research articles and case studies on all aspects of rical research articles and case studies on all aspects of mental health policy and administration. Refereed by academics and practitioners; 6 months for editorial decision; 6 months to publish; 30% accepted for publication.

314. *Administration in Social Work.* 1977. 4. Index.
     Simon Slavin. School of Social Administration, Temple
     University, Philadelphia, Pennsylvania 19122.

This quarterly publication, oriented toward an audience of social work administrators, is devoted to management and administration in social work and the human services. It also covers topics in the related fields of social and public policy. Refereed by academics and practitioners; 3½ months for editorial decision; 6-10 months to publish; 25% accepted for publication.

315. *Community Mental Health Journal.* 1964. 4. Index.
     James A. Ciarlo and Herbert Diamond. 2233 Wisconsin
     Avenue, N. W., Washington, D. C. 20007.

Sponsored by the National Council of Community Mental
Health Centers, this journal, for individuals involved in any
aspect of community mental health, is devoted to the broad fields
of community mental health theory, practice, and research.
Articles focus on community mental health programs, treatment
techniques, and the community environment in which they operate.
Refereed by academics and practitioners; 3-4 months for editorial decision; 7-8 months to publish; 20% accepted for publication.

316. *Evaluation and the Health Professions.* 1978. 4.
     R. Barker Bausell and Carolyn F. Waltz. School of
     Nursing, University of Maryland, 655 W. Lombard Street,
     Baltimore, Maryland 21201.

This publication is designed for all health professionals
interested or engaged in the development, implementation, and
evaluation of health programs. The focus is on evaluation
studies, developments in professional education, methodological
techniques, and the philosophy and politics of evaluation.
Refereed by academics and practitioners; 2-3 months for editorial decision; 6 months to publish; 30% accepted for publication.

317. *Health and Social Work.* 1976. 4. Index. Rosalie A.
     Kane. National Association of Social Workers, Editorial
     Office, 2 Park Avenue, New York, New York 10016.

Sponsored by NASW, this quarterly journal, for social
workers and other professionals in health care, covers all
aspects of physical and mental health that are of concern to
social workers, such as descriptions of practice, innovations
and research, client and community legislation, and social
policy and planning. Refereed by academics and practitioners;
3 months for editorial decision; 6 months to 1 year to publish;
23% accepted for publication.

318. *International Review of Community Development.* 1958.
     2. Cum. Ind. Frédéric Lesemann. International Forum
     of Community Development, Ecole de service social CP
     6128, Université de Montreal, Montreal, Quebec
     H3C 3J7, Canada.

The *International Review* is a bi-annual journal,
written in both French and English. Articles deal with issues
in adult education, public and community health, community

development, and social community work.

319. *International Social Security Review*. 1968. 4. Index.
   International Social Security Association, Case postale
   1, CH-1211, Geneva 22, Switzerland.

   Published in English, French, and German, this quarterly
publication contains articles on social security policy and
administration, particularly of a comparative nature, and news
of social security legislation. Its intended audience is
social security administrators, social policy-makers, scholars
and students in the field of social policy. Topics covered
include pensions, sickness insurance, health care, maternity,
work injury, occupational diseases, unemployment, family allow-
ances, social services, welfare, rehabilitation, and accident
prevention. Secretary General of the ISSA decides; 3-4 months
for editorial decision; 6-9 months to be published; 30-40%
accepted for publication.

320. *Journal of Applied Behavior Analysis*. 1967. 4. Index.
   Cum. Ind. David Barlow, Department of Psychology,
   State University of New York, Albany, New York 12222.

   Published by the Society for the Experimental Analysis
of Behavior, this scholarly journal is aimed toward an audience of psychologists, psychiatrists, physicians, educators,
and social workers. It publishes reports of experimental research involving applications of the experimental analysis of
behavior to problems of social importance. Refereed by academics; 2-2½ months for editorial decision; 6 months to publish;
30% accepted for publication.

321. *Journal of Community Health*. 1974. 4. Robert L. Kane,
   M.D. c/o The Rand Corporation, 1700 Main Street,
   Santa Monica, California 90406.

   Sponsored by the Association of Teachers of Preventive
Medicine, this quarterly publication for academics and practitioners in health care features articles on health care delivery, preventive medicine, and the use of health care.
Refereed by academics and practitioners; 3 months for editorial
decision; 6 months to publish; 25% accepted for publication.

322. *Journal of Gerontology*. 1945. 6. Index. Harold Brody.
   317 Farber Hall, State University of New York, Buffalo,
   New York 14214.

   This bi-monthly journal of the Gerontological Society
publishes articles in the biomedical, medical, psychological,

and social sciences, dealing with a broad range of topics in
the study of the process of aging and the problems of aged
people. Refereed by academics; 2 months for editorial decision;
4-6 months to publish; 25% accepted for publication.

323. *Journal of Health and Human Resources Administration.*
      1977. 4. Index. Cum. Ind. Jack Rabin and Thomas
      Vocino. Department of Government, Auburn University
      at Montgomery, Montgomery, Alabama   36117.

      Sponsored by the Southern Public Administration Educa-
tion Foundation, this quarterly journal publishes articles of
a general nature on all aspects of health administration and
human services administration. Refereed by academics and
practitioners; 1½ months for editorial decision; 1-10 months
to publish; 15-20% accepted for publication.

324. *Journal of Health and Social Behavior.* 1960. 4.
      Index. Cum. Ind. Howard B. Kaplan. Department of
      Psychiatry, Baylor University College of Medicine,
      1200 Mousund Avenue, Houston, Texas   77030.

      A publication of the American Sociological Association,
this journal publishes reports of empirical studies, theoretical analyses, and synthesizing reviews that employ a sociological perspective to clarify aspects of social life bearing
on human health and illness, both physical and mental. The
scope includes studies of the organizations, institutions,
and occupations devoted to health services as well as studies
of the behavior of actual and potential recipients of these
services. Refereed by academics; 7 weeks for editorial decision;
3-6 months to publish; 10% accepted for publication.

325. *Journal of Social Issues.* 1945. 4. Joseph F. McGrath.
      Department of Psychology, University of Illinois,
      Champaign, Illinois   61820.

      The *Journal of Social Issues* is published quarterly by
the Society for the Psychological Study of Social Issues.
Each issue is organized around one unifying theme or topic.
JSI's goal is to communicate scientific findings and interpre-
tations regarding social issues in a non-technical manner.
Refereed by academics; 8-10 months for editorial decision;
24 months to publish; % accepted not available.

326. *Journal of Social Policy.* 1972. 4. Index. Robert
      Pinker. London School of Economics and Political Science,
      Houghton Street, London WC2A 2AE, England.

This is the quarterly journal of the Social Administration Association, covering all subjects relevant to the study of social policy and administration. Articles on social policy include historical and theoretical analyses, as well as studies of processes and problems of implementation of national and local social policies. Social administration topics are approached from a variety of social science, social work and social action perspectives. Refereed by academics and practitioners; 5 months for editorial decision; 6-8 months to publish; 20% accepted for publication.

327. *Journal of Social Welfare.* 1973. 3. Edward A. Dutton. School of Social Welfare, 308 Twente Hall, University of Kansas, Lawrence, Kansas 66045.

The *Journal of Social Welfare* is a journal for practitioners, educators and students in the field of social welfare. It strives to act as "a platform for innovative ideas and practice" in the fields of social work and social welfare. Refereed by academics and practitioners; 3 months for editorial decision; 3-6 months to publish; 50% accepted for publication.

328. *New England Journal of Human Services.* 1980. 4. W. Robert Curtis and Mark R. Yessian. P. O. Box 9167, Boston, Massachusetts 02114.

A recently established journal for human services managers and scholars interested in human services issues, this practitioner-oriented quarterly publication seeks to provide an interdisciplinary forum for improving approaches to the management and delivery of human services during an era of severe budgetary limitations. Subject fields include health, mental health, social services, and education. Refereed by academics and practitioners; 1½-2 months for editorial decision; 3-6 months to publish; % accepted not available.

329. *Public Health Reports.* 1879. 6. Index. Marian Priest Tebben. Health Resources Administration, Department of Health and Human Services, 10-30 Center Building, 3700 East-West Highway, Hyattsville, Maryland 20782.

This bi-monthly journal publishes scientific papers concerned with the delivery of health services and the many facets of health care, as well as technical reports documenting studies and reports of basic and applied research. Its subject fields include epidemiology, health planning and health economics, and community medicine. Refereed by academics and practitioners; 3 months for editorial decision; 8-10 months to publish; 33% accepted for publication.

330. *Social Casework: The Journal of Contemporary Social
      Work*. 1920. 4. Index. Jacqueline Marx Atkins.
      44 East 23rd Street, New York, New York 10010.

Sponsored by the Family Service Association of America,
Social Casework publishes articles of interest to a broad audience of professional social workers, educators and others who
are concerned about social problems, social action, problems of
interpersonal relationships and social functioning. Its subject fields include social work theory, education, practice,
and administration; social welfare and social policy; and
social action and research. Refereed by academics and practitioners; 3 months for editorial decision; 6-12 months to publish; 20% accepted for publication.

331. *Social Service Review*. 1927. 4. Index. Cum. Ind.
      Frank Breul. 969 E. 60th Street, Chicago, Illinois
      60637.

This journal, for social work practitioners, social
scientists, and human service professionals, is devoted to the
objective study of social welfare organizations, policies, and
practices. It publishes articles concerning poverty, ethnicity,
social welfare policy, income distribution, mental health services, social administration, and community development.
Refereed by academics and practitioners; 3 months for editorial
decision; 6 months to publish; 20% accepted for publication.

332. *Social Work*. 1956. Index. Anne Minahan. National
      Association of Social Workers, 2 Park Avenue, New York,
      New York 10016.

Social Work is the official journal of the National
Association of Social Workers. Committed to "improving practice and extending knowledge in the field of social work," the
journal publishes articles on theory, practice, and current
issues in social work for an audience of social work practitioners, academicians, and students. Refereed by academics
and practitioners; 3 months for editorial decision; 6-9 months
to publish; 14-18% accepted for publication.

XIV. URBAN ADMINISTRATION

333. *Journal of the American Planning Association*. 1935. 4.
      Index. Kenneth Pearlman. Department of City and Region-
      al Planning, Ohio State University, 190 W. 17th Avenue,
      Columbus, Ohio 43210.

This is an academic research publication in the field
of urban and regional planning for practicing planners,
academics in planning and related fields, and government officials. Refereed by academics and practitioners; 1-2 months
for editorial decision; 3-4 months to publish; 23% accepted
for publication.

334. *Journal of the American Real Estate and Urban Economics
     Association.* 1967. 4. Index. William B. Brueggeman.
     American Real Estate and Urban Economics Association,
     Edwin L. Cox School of Business, Southern Methodist
     University, Dallas, Texas 75275.

This scholarly journal, intended for academicians, professional consultants and government officials, specializes
in research on real estate, housing, land economics, public
finance, taxation and urban planning. Refereed by academics;
2 months for editorial decision; 9 months to publish; 20%
accepted for publication.

335. *Journal of Housing.* 1944. 11. Index. Frederic M.
     Voselang. National Association of Housing and Redevelop-
     ment Officials, 2600 Virginia Avenue, N. W., Washington,
     D. C. 20037.

Published by NAHRO, the *Journal of Housing* is directed
toward an audience of public officials, private developers,
housing finance officers, and planners. It features analytical
articles on national housing and urban affairs policy; assisted
housing management and development; community and economic
development; city rebuilding; and neighborhood conservation.
Editor decides; 3 weeks for editorial decision; 2 months to
publish; 40% accepted for publication.

336. *Journal of Urban Affairs.* 1978. 4. Patricia Klobus
     Edwards. Division of Environmental and Urban Systems,
     Virginia Polytechnic Institute and State University,
     Blacksburg, Virginia 24061.

Formerly the *Urban Affairs Papers*, this quarterly journal is sponsored by the Urban Affairs Association. Its purpose
is to publish articles related to urban research and policy
analysis of interest to a broad audience of scholars and practitioners. Refereed by academics and practitioners; 3 months
for editorial decision; 3-6 months to publish; 10% accepted for
publication.

337. *Journal of Urban Analysis.* 1972. 2. Index. Stan
     Altman. Institute of Public Services Performance,
     183 Madison Avenue, Suite 419, New York, New York 10016.

This journal focuses on policy research, oriented broadly toward urban problems. Drawing upon the fields of engineering, planning, operations research, and the social and behavioral sciences, its articles typically deal with such diverse topic
areas as fire protection, refuse collection and disposal, power
plant location and environmental impacts, municipal finance,
regulatory legislation, the criminal justice system, housing,
and welfare. Refereed by academics and practitioners; 2-4
months for editorial decision; 3-6 months to publish; 50%
accepted for publication.

338. *Local Authority Administration.* 1975. 2. G. W. A.
     Bush. Institute of Local Authority Administration,
     P. O. Box 278, Wellington, New Zealand.

Published by the Institute, this periodical covers
current topics of interest in local government administration,
with an emphasis on management in New Zealand local government.
Its primary intended audience is local government administrators. Editors and advisory committee decide; 1 month for
editorial decision; 2-5 months to publish; 85-90% accepted for
publication.

339. *Local Government Studies.* 1971. 6. Alan Norton.
     Institute of Local Government Studies, J. G. Smith
     Building, University of Birmingham, Birmingham B15 2TT,
     England.

This bi-monthly journal publishes research-based, theoretical and issue-oriented articles related to the field of
problems in and related to local government and administration,
with the purpose of acting as a forum for interchange of knowledge and ideas among academics and practitioners. While most
of its articles relate to local government in Britain, the
journal does publish papers concerned with research findings
and developments in other industrialized countries. Refereed
by academics and practitioners; 1-3 months for editorial
decision; 6-12 months to publish; 30% accepted for publication.

340. *Municipal Review.* 1930. 12. Index. Peter Smith.
     Association of Metropolitan Authorities, 36 Old Queen
     Street, London SW1, England.

This journal, for metropolitan local authorities, publishes articles on local authority activities including housing,
finance, planning, transportation, urban renewal, industrial
regeneration, central-local government relations, education,
and social services. Editor decides; time for editorial decision
not stated; 3 months to publish; articles are generally solicited.

341. *Planning*. 1972. 12. Sylvia Lewis. American Planning
      Association, 1313 E. 60th Street, Chicago, Illinois 60637.

This monthly publication of the American Planning Association carries articles about urban affairs and urban regional
planning dealing with a wide range of topics within the neighborhood development field, specifically land use, housing, transportation, and energy. It is intended for city planners, teachers and students of planning, consultants and laymen interested
in the field. Editors decide; 1 month to editorial decision; 2-6
months to publish; 20% accepted for publication.

342. *Town and Country Planning*. 1904. 12. Index. D. R.
      Diamond. Town and Country Planning Association, 17
      Carlton House Terrace, London SW1Y 5AS, England.

This is a monthly publication for professionals in planning, government policy-makers, and academicians. It publishes
brief articles dealing with comments on and policies for town
and country planning, social development, and urbanization in
Britain and elsewhere, with special reference to new towns/new
communities. Editor decides; 1½-2 months for editorial decision;
1-10 months to publish; 50% accepted for publication.

343. *Town Planning Review*. 1910. 4. Index. Cum. Ind.
      in preparation. Dr. David W. Massey. Department of
      Civic Design, University of Liverpool, P. O. Box 147,
      Liverpool L69 3BX, England.

The *Review* publishes articles on urban and regional
planning, including rural planning, transportation planning,
social planning, public policy-making, and urban and landscape
design. Refereed by academics and practitioners; 3-6 months
for editorial decision; 6-9 months to publish; 25-30% accepted
for publication.

344. *Urban Anthropology*. 1972. 4. Index. Dr. Jack R.
      Rollwagen. Department of Anthropology, State University
      of New York College at Brockport, Brockport, New York
      14420.

Sponsored by the Institute for the Study of Man, *Urban
Anthropology* publishes scholarly articles by anthropologists
and other related social and behavioral scientists on the cultural systems of cities, and city-related topics. Refereed by
academics; 1½-3 months for editorial decision; 6 months to publish; 33% accepted for publication.

345. *Urban Land*. 1941. 12. Index. W. Paul O'Mara.
      Urban Land Institute, 1200 18th Street, N. W., Washington,
      D. C. 20036.

This ULI monthly publication is intended for a broad
audience of planners and others interested in current issues
and trends in land development and planning. It publishes short
articles on such topics as housing, land use planning, property
development, and public-private sector relationships. Editor
decides; 1 month for editorial decision; 1-3 months to publish;
35% accepted for publication.

346. *Urban Life*. 1971. 4. James Thomas. Department of
     Sociology, Northern Illinois University, DeKalb, Illinois
     60115.

Urban Life publishes articles dealing with qualitative,
especially ethnographic, research on topics of social structure,
social interaction, and other areas of social organization.
Refereed by academics and practitioners; $2\frac{1}{2}$-$3\frac{1}{2}$ months for
editorial decision; 8-12 months to publish; 12% accepted for
publication.

347. *The Urban Review: Issues and Ideas in Public Education*.
     1965. 4. Index. David E. Kapel and William T. Pink.
     College of Education, University of Nebraska, Omaha,
     Nebraska 68132.

The *Review* seeks to provide a forum for both empirical
studies and theoretical essays concerning schooling in an urban
setting. Its articles deal with all aspects of education in
the urban community. Refereed by academics; 2 months for
editorial decision; 3-6 months to publish; % accepted not available.

348. *Urban Studies*. 1964. 3. Index. Roger Vaughan.
     Economics Department, Citibank, 399 Park Avenue, New York,
     New York 10043.

This is an international journal dealing with socio-
economic issues relating to urban and regional planning and
development. Its articles include contributions from the
fields of economics, sociology, economic geography, planning,
and econometric modeling. Refereed by academics and practitioners; 3 months for editorial decision; 9-12 months to publish; 15-20% accepted for publication.

4.
a select bibliography
of books in
American public administration

4. A SELECT BIBLIOGRAPHY OF AMERICAN PUBLIC ADMINISTRATION

Gerald E. Caiden

A specialized library at a renowned research university or a public professional organization contains tens of thousands of references in many languages. To read them all is a lifetime's work. This chapter is designed for readers who do not have the time or opportunity to search out source material for themselves. It concentrates on books published in the United States and written by persons residing in the country. It excludes books written by nonresidents about American public administration or published outside the United States, which are generally inaccessible to readers in this country. It is divided into six self-explanatory sections. The first (Items 349-443) consists of about 95 books, arranged chronologically, published between 1890 and 1960 which have since been recognized as essential reading. They continue to appear in reading lists; they remain for the most part in print. The second section (Items 444-587) contains a compilation of core texts in public administration, also arranged chronologically to help readers trace the history of the discipline and keep up to date on the latest editions. The next two sections do the same for general anthologies (Items 588-670), and bibliographies, case studies and workbooks (Items 671-705). The fifth section (Items 706-885) consists of about two hundred of the most frequently cited contemporary texts that accompany the core texts which draw heavily on them. The last section (Items 886-1220) consists of twelve lists of more specialized volumes that supplement more general reading. Selection has been based on relevance to current trends, originality of content, and available circulation figures to date.

I. CLASSIC TEXTS IN AMERICAN PUBLIC ADMINISTRATION 1890-1960

American public administration dates from the publication in 1887 of Woodrow Wilson's seminal essay "The Study of Admin-

istration," in Volume 2 of *Political Science Quarterly*, although
it had been preceded by several commentaries on American public
administration, such as *The Federalist Papers* (1788) and
de Toqueville's *Democracy in America* (1834). But it was
Wilson who maintained that the study of public administration
could and should be separate from the study of politics, and
that a science of American public administration was possible.
Since then, many studies along these lines have followed in
accelerating volume. Several have achieved the status of classi-
cal studies either because they constitute pathfinding landmark
publications or because their originality has influenced succeed-
ing works and they have been quoted frequently ever since. The
following is a selective list of such classics published before
1961.

349. Goodnow, F. J., *Politics and Administration*, New York,
      Macmillan, also Russell and Russell (1967). 1900.

350. Taylor, F. W., *The Principles of Scientific Management*,
      New York, Harper. 1911.

351. White, L. D., *Introduction to the Study of Public Admin-
      istration*, New York, Macmillan. 1926.

352. Dewey, J., *The Public and Its Problems*, New York, Holt.
      1927.

353. White, L. D., *The City Manager*, Chicago, University of
      Chicago Press. 1927.

354. Stewart, F., *The National Civil Service Reform League*,
      Austin, The University of Texas Press. 1929.

355. Beck, J. M., *Our Wonderland of Bureaucracy*, New York,
      Macmillan. 1932.

356. Friedrich, C. J., and Cole, T., *Responsible Bureaucracy*,
      Cambridge, MA, Harvard University Press. 1932.

357. Mayo, E., *The Human Problems of an Industrial Civiliza-
      tion*, New York, The Viking Press. 1933.

358. Merriam, C., et al., *Better Government Personnel*, New
      York, McGraw-Hill. 1935.

359. Tead, O., *The Art of Leadership*, New York, McGraw-Hill.
      1935.

360. Wilmerding, L., *Government by Merit*, New York, McGraw-Hill. 1935.

361. Gaus, J. M., et al., *The Frontiers of Public Administration*, Chicago, University of Chicago Press. 1936.

362. Herring, E. P., *Public Administration and the Public Interest*, New York, McGraw-Hill. 1936.

363. Kingsley, J., and Mosher, W. E., *Public Personnel Administration*, New York, Harper. 1936.

364. Gulick, L., and Urwick, L., *Papers on the Science of Administration*, New York, Institute of Public Administration, Columbia University. 1937.

365. Barnard, C. I., *The Functions of the Executive*, Cambridge, MA, Harvard University Press. 1938.

366. Landis, J. M., *The Administrative Process*, New Haven, CT, Yale University Press. 1938.

367. Ridley, C. E., and Simon, H. A., *Measuring Municipal Activities*, Chicago, International City Management Association. 1938.

368. Mooney, J. D., *The Principles of Organization*, New York, Harper. 1939.

369. Roethlisberger, F. J., and Dickson, W. J., *Management and the Worker*, Cambridge, MA, Harvard University Press. 1939.

370. Follett, M. P., *Dynamic Administration* (collected papers edited by E. M. Fox and L. Urwick), New York, Hippocrene Books. 1940.

371. Pfiffner, J. M., *Municipal Administration*, New York, The Ronald Press. 1940.

372. Pfiffner, J. M., *Research Methods in Public Administration*, New York, The Ronald Press. 1940.

373. Baruch, I., *Position Classification in the Public Service*, Chicago, Public Personnel Association. 1941.

374. Beard, C. A., *Public Policy and General Welfare*, New Haven, CT, Yale University Press. 1941.

375. Burnham, J., *The Managerial Revolution*, Westport, CT, Greenwood Press. 1941.

376. Wallace, S. C., *Federal Decentralization*, New York, Columbia University Press. 1941.

377. Leiserson, A., *Administrative Regulation*, Chicago, University of Chicago Press. 1942.

378. Hayek, F. A., *The Road to Serfdom*, Chicago, University of Chicago Press. 1944.

379. Kingsley, J. D., *Representative Bureaucracy*, Yellow Springs, OH, The Antioch Press. 1944.

380. Lilienthal, D. E., *T. V. A.-Democracy on the March*, New York, Harper and Row. 1944.

381. Von Mises, L., *Bureaucracy*, New Haven, CT, Yale University Press. 1944.

382. Appleby, P. H., *Big Democracy*, New York, Knopf. 1945.

383. Dimock, M. E., *The Executive in Action*, New York, Harper and Row. 1945.

384. Leighton, A. H., *The Governing of Men*, Princeton, NJ, Princeton University Press. 1945.

385. Lewin, K., *A Dynamic Theory of Personality*, New York, McGraw-Hill. 1945.

386. Tead, O., *Democratic Administration*, New York, Association Press. 1945.

387. Marx, F. M., ed., *Elements of Public Administration*, Englewood Cliffs, NJ, Prentice-Hall. 1946.

388. Gaus, J. M., *Reflections on Public Administration*, University, AL, University of Alabama Press. 1947.

389. Gerth, H. H., and Mills, C. W., *From Max Weber*, New York, Oxford University Press. 1947.

390. Henderson, A. M., and Parsons, T., eds., *Max Weber: The Theory of Social and Economic Organization*, Glencoe, IL, The Free Press. 1947.

391. Simon, H. A., *Administrative Behavior*, New York, Macmillan. 1947.

392. Waldo, D., *The Administrative State*, New York, Ronald Press. 1948.

393. White, L. D., *The Federalists*, New York, Macmillan. 1948.

394. Appleby, P. H., *Policy and Administration*, University, AL, University of Alabama Press. 1949.

395. Fesler, J. W., *Area and Administration*, University, AL, University of Alabama Press. 1949.

396. Lepawsky, A., ed., *Administration*, New York, Knopf. 1949.

397. McLean, J., *Public Service and University Education*, Princeton, NJ, Princeton University Press. 1949.

398. Selznick, P., *TVA and the Grass Roots*, New York, Harper and Row. 1949.

399. Emmerich, H., *Essays on Federal Reorganization*, University, AL, University of Alabama Press. 1950.

400. Hyneman, C., *Bureaucracy in a Democracy*, New York, Harper. 1950.

401. Simon, H. A., et al., *Public Administration*, New York, Knopf. 1950.

402. Maass, A., *Muddy Waters*, Cambridge, MA, Harvard University Press. 1951.

403. Mills, C. W., *White Collar*, New York, Oxford University Press. 1951.

404. Truman, D., *The Governmental Process*, New York, Knopf. 1951.

405. White, L. D., *The Jeffersonians*, New York, Macmillan. 1951.

406. Appleby, P. H., *Morality and Administration in Democratic Government*, Baton Rouge, LA, Louisiana State University Press. 1952.

407. Leys, W. A. R., *Ethics for Policy Decisions*, Englewood Cliffs, NJ, Prentice-Hall. 1952.

408. Merton, R. K., et al., eds., *Reader in Bureaucracy*, Glencoe, IL, Free Press. 1952.

409. Stein, H., ed., *Public Administration and Policy Development*, New York, Harcourt, Brace and Jovanovich. 1952.

410. Drucker, P. F., *The Practice of Management*, New York, Harper and Row. 1954.

411. Maslow, A. H., *Motivation and Personality*, New York, Harper and Row. 1954.

412. Millett, J. D., *Management in the Public Service*, New York, McGraw-Hill. 1954.

413. Price, D. K., *Government and Science*, New York, New York University Press. 1954.

414. White, L. D., *The Jacksonians*, New York, Macmillan. 1954.

415. Bernstein, M. H., *Regulating Business by Independent Commission*, Princeton, NJ, Princeton University Press. 1955.

416. Blau, P. M., *The Dynamics of Bureaucracy*, Chicago, University of Chicago Press. 1955.

417. Burkhead, J., *Government Budgeting*, New York, Wiley. 1955.

418. Meyerson, M., and Banfield, E. C., *Politics, Planning and the Public Interest*, New York, The Free Press. 1955.

419. Waldo, D., *Perspectives on Administration*, University, AL, University of Alabama Press. 1955.

420. Barnett, H. G., *Anthropology in Administration*, Evanston, IL, Row, Peterson. 1956.

421. Blau, P. M., *Bureaucracy in Modern Society*, New York, Random House. 1956.

422. Downs, A., *An Economic Theory of Democracy*, New York, Harper and Row. 1957.

423. Marx, F. M., *The Administrative State*, Chicago, University of Chicago Press. 1957.

424. Selznick, P., *Leadership in Administration*, New York, Row, Peterson. 1957.

425. Siffin, W. J., ed., *Toward the Comparative Study of Public Administration*, Bloomington, IN, Indiana University Press. 1957.

426. Galbraith, J. K., *The Affluent Society*, Boston, Houghton Mifflin. 1958.

427. McKean, R. N., *Efficiency in Government Through Systems Analysis*, New York, Wiley. 1958.

428. March, J. G., and Simon, H. A., *Organizations*, New York, Wiley. 1958.

429. Redford, E. S., *Ideal and Practice in Public Administration*, University, AL, University of Alabama Press. 1958.

430. Van Riper, P. P., *History of the United States Civil Service*, Evanston, IL, Row, Peterson. 1958.

431. White, L. D., *The Republican Era*, New York, Macmillan. 1958.

432. Dimock, M. E., *Administrative Vitality*, New York, Harper and Row. 1959.

433. Herzberg, F., et al., *The Motivation to Work*, New York, Wiley. 1959.

434. Hitch, C. J., and McKean, R. N., *The Economics of Defense in the Nuclear Age*, Cambridge, MA, Harvard University Press. 1960.

435. Kaufman, H., *The Forest Ranger*, Baltimore, The Johns Hopkins University Press. 1960.

436. McGregor, D., *The Human Side of Enterprise*, New York, McGraw-Hill. 1960.

437. Neustadt, R., *Presidential Power*, New York, Wiley. 1960.

438. Pfiffner, J. M., and Sherwood, F., *Administrative Organization*, Englewood Cliffs, NJ, Prentice-Hall. 1960.

439. Sayre, W. S., and Kaufman, H., *Governing New York City*,
      New York, Russell Sage Foundation. 1960.

440. Schubert, G., *The Public Interest*, Glencoe, IL, Free
      Press. 1960.

441. Simon, H. A., *The New Science of Management Decision*,
      New York, Harper and Row. 1960.

442. Tussman, J., *Obligation and the Body Politic*, New York,
      Oxford University Press. 1960.

443. Wolin, S. S., *Politics and Vision*, Boston, Little Brown.
      1960.

II.   CORE TEXTS IN AMERICAN PUBLIC ADMINISTRATION

Some core texts trace their first editions before World
War II and a comparison of successive editions would provide
an interesting commentary on recent shifts in disciplinary
emphasis. Most have appeared in the last decade or so as newcomers seek to replace the dominant position once held by
Leonard White, John Pfiffner, Morstein Marx and even Herbert
Simon, Dwight Waldo, John Millett, and Marshall Dimock. Each
text has its own special characteristics in style, treatment,
sources, values, emphasis and linkages. They vary considerably in length, quality, readability and cost. Unfortunately,
textbooks are not normally reviewed by journals in the profession. See, however, James S. Bowman, "The Readability of
Introductory Textbooks in Public Administration," *Administrative Science Quarterly*, 22 (June 1977), 373-376; his "Introductory Textbooks in Public Administration," *Midwest Review
of Public Administration*, 12 (September 1978), 205-208; and
occasional textbook review essays in the *Public Administration Review*.

444. White, L. D., *Introduction to the Study of Public Ad-
      ministration*, New York, Macmillan. 1926.

445. Willoughby, W. F., *Principles of Public Administration*,
      Baltimore, MD, The Johns Hopkins University Press.
      1927.

446. Pfiffner, J. M., *Public Administration*, New York,
      Ronald Press. 1935.

447. Kingsley, J. D., and Mosher, W. E., *Public Personnel Administration*, New York, Harper. 1936.

448. Walker, H., *Public Administration in the United States*, New York, Farrar and Rinehart. 1937.

449. White, L. D., (1926), Second Edition. 1939.

450. Kingsley and Mosher (1936), Second Edition. 1941.

451. Marx, F. M., ed., *Elements of Public Administration*, New York, Prentice-Hall. 1946.

452. Pfiffner, J. M., and Presthus, R. V., (1935), Second Edition. 1946.

453. White, L. D., (1939), Third Edition. 1948.

454. Graves, W. B., *Public Administration in a Democratic Society*, Boston, Heath, 1950.

455. Kingsley, Mosher, and Stahl, G., (1941), Third Edition. 1950.

456. Simon, H. A., Smithburg, D., and Thompson, V. A., *Public Administration*, New York, Knopf. 1950.

457. Charlesworth, J. C., *Governmental Administration*, New York, Harper. 1951.

458. Dimock, M. E., and Dimock, G. O., *Public Administration*, New York, Rinehart. 1953.

459. Pfiffner and Presthus, (1946), Third Edition. 1953.

460. Torpey, W. G., *Public Personnel Management*, New York, Van Nostrand. 1953.

461. Millett, J. D., *Management in the Public Service*, New York, McGraw-Hill. 1954.

462. Seckler-Hudson, C., *Organization and Management*, Washington, DC, American University Press. 1955.

463. Waldo, D., *The Study of Public Administration*, Garden City, NY, Doubleday. 1955.

464. White, L. D., (1948), Fourth Edition. 1955.

465. Powell, N. J., *Personnel Administration in Government*, Englewood Cliffs, NJ, Prentice-Hall. 1956.

466. Stahl, G., (1950), Fourth Edition. 1956.

467. Marx, F. M., *The Administrative State*, Chicago, University of Chicago Press. 1957.

468. Dimock and Dimock (1953), Second Edition, Holt, Rinehart and Winston. 1958.

469. Bartholomew, P. C., *Public Administration*, Paterson, NJ, Littlefield, Adams. 1959.

470. Marx, F. M., ed., (1946), Second Edition. 1959.

471. Millett, J. D., *Government and Public Administration*, New York, Holt, Rinehart and Winston. 1959.

472. Nigro, F. A., *Public Personnel Administration*, New York, Holt, Rinehart and Winston. 1959.

473. Pfiffner and Presthus (1955), Fourth Edition. 1960.

474. Pfiffner, J. M., and Sherwood, F., *Administrative Organization*, Englewood Cliffs, NJ, Prentice-Hall. 1960.

475. Emmerich, H. A., *A Handbook of Public Administration*, New York, United Nations. 1961.

476. Waldo, D., (1955), Second Edition, New York, Random House. 1961.

477. Stahl, G., (1956), Fifth Edition. 1962.

478. Corson, J. J., and Harris, J. P., *Public Administration in Modern Society*, New York, McGraw-Hill. 1963.

479. Dimock, Dimock and Koenig, L. W., (1958), Third Edition. 1964.

480. Graves, W. B., *American Intergovernmental Relations*, New York, Scribner. 1964.

481. Wildavsky, A., *The Politics of Budgetary Process*, Boston, Little, Brown. 1964.

482. Nigro, F. A., *Modern Public Administration*, New York, Harper and Row. 1965.

483. Presthus, R. V., *Behavioral Approaches to Public Administration*, University, AL, University of Alabama Press. 1965.

484. Heady, F. C., *Public Administration: A Comparative Perspective*, Englewood Cliffs, NJ, Prentice-Hall. 1966.

485. Henderson, K. M., *Emerging Synthesis in American Public Administration*, New York, Asia Publishing House. 1966.

486. Jacob, C. E., *Policy and Bureaucracy*, Princeton, NJ, Van Nostrand. 1966.

487. Millett, J. D., *Organization for the Public Service*, Princeton, NJ, Van Nostrand. 1966.

488. Bartholomew, P. C., (1959), Second Edition. 1967.

489. Pfiffner and Presthus (1960), Fifth Edition. 1967.

490. Buechner, J. C., *Public Administration*, Belmont, CA, Dickenson. 1968.

491. Charlesworth, J. C., ed., *Theory and Practice of Public Administration*, Philadelphia, A. A. P. S. S. 1968.

492. Mosher, F. C., *Democracy and the Public Service*, New York, Oxford University Press. 1968.

493. Berkley, G. E., *The Administrative Revolution*, Englewood Cliffs, NJ, Prentice-Hall. 1969.

494. Dimock, Dimock, and Koenig (1964), Fourth Edition. 1969.

495. Gawthrop, L. C., *Bureaucratic Behavior in the Executive Branch*, New York, Free Press. 1969.

496. Hodgson, J. S., *Public Administration*, New York, McGraw-Hill. 1969.

497. Redford, E. S., *Democracy in the Administrative State*, New York, Oxford University Press. 1969.

498. Davis, J. W., *The National Executive Branch*, New York,
      Free Press. 1970.

499. Nigro, F. A., (1965), Second Edition. 1970.

500. Sharkansky, I., *Public Administration*, Chicago, Markham.
      1970.

501. Caiden, G. E., *The Dynamics of Public Administration*,
      New York, Holt, Rinehart and Winston. 1971.

502. Gawthrop, L. C., *Administrative Politics and Social
      Change*, New York, St. Martin's Press. 1971.

503. Marini, F., ed., *Toward a New Public Administration*,
      Scranton, PA, Chandler. 1971.

504. Stahl, G., (1962), Sixth Edition. 1971.

505. Waldo, D., ed., *Public Administration in a Time of
      Turbulence*, Scranton, PA, Chandler. 1971.

506. Bartholomew, P. C., (1967), Third Edition. 1972.

507. Dye, T. R., *Understanding Public Policy*, Englewood Cliffs,
      NJ, Prentice-Hall. 1972.

508. Sharkansky, I., (1970), Second Edition, Rand McNally.
      1972.

509. Allensworth, D. T., *Public Administration*, Philadelphia,
      Lippincott. 1973.

510. Nigro, F. A., and Nigro, L. G., (1970), Third Edition.
      1973.

511. Ostrom, V., *The Intellectual Crisis in American Public
      Administration*, University, AL, University of Alabama
      Press. 1973.

512. Rehfuss, J., *Public Administration as Political Pro-
      cess*, New York, Scribner. 1973.

513. Davis, J. W., *Politics, Policy and Bureaucracy*,
      New York, Free Press. 1974.

514. Wildavsky, A., (1964), Second Edition. 1974.

515. Woll, P., *Public Policy*, Cambridge, MA, Winthrop. 1974.

516. Anderson, J. E., *Public Policy Making*, New York, Praeger. 1975.

517. Berkley, G. E., *The Craft of Public Administration*, Allyn and Bacon. 1975.

518. Cayer, N. J., *Public Personnel Administration in the United States*, New York, St. Martin's Press. 1975.

519. Henry, N. L., *Public Administration and Public Affairs*, Englewood Cliffs, NJ, Prentice-Hall. 1975.

520. Morrow, W. L., *Public Administration*, New York, Random House. 1975.

521. Presthus, R. V., (1967), Sixth Edition. 1975.

522. Sharkansky, I., (1972), Third Edition. 1975.

523. Fried, R. C., *Performance in American Bureaucracy*, Boston, Little Brown. 1976.

524. Lutrin, C. E., and Settle, A. K., *American Public Administration*, Palo Alto, CA, Mayfield. 1976.

525. Nigro, F. A., and Nigro, L. G., *The New Public Personnel Administration*. Itasca, IL, Peacock. 1976.

526. Richardson, I. L., and Baldwin, S., *Public Administration*, Columbus, OH, Merrill. 1976.

527. Robbins, S. P., *The Administrative Process*, Englewood Cliffs, NJ, Prentice-Hall. 1976.

528. Buchele, R. B., *The Management of Business and Public Organizations*, New York, McGraw-Hill. 1977.

529. Dvorin, F. P., and Simmons, R. H., *Public Administration*, New York, Alfred. 1977.

530. Golembiewski, R. T., *Public Administration as a Developing Discipline*, New York, Dekker. 1977.

531. Gortner, H. F., *Administration in the Public Sector*, New York, Wiley. 1977.

532. Kramer, F. A., *Dynamics of Public Bureaucracy*,
     Cambridge, MA, Winthrop. 1977.

533. McCurdy, H. E., *Public Administration*, Menlo Park,
     CA, Cummings. 1977.

534. Medeiros, J. A., and Schmitt, D. E., *Public Bureaucracy:
     Values and Perspectives*, North Scituate, MA, Duxbury
     Press. 1977.

535. Nigro, F. A., and Nigro, L. C., (1973), Fourth Edition.
     1977.

536. Starling, G., *Managing the Public Sector*, Homewood,
     IL, Dorsey. 1977.

537. Berkley, G. E., (1975), Second Edition. 1978.

538. Bower, J. L., and Christenson, C. J., *Public Management:
     Text and Cases*, Englewood Cliffs, NJ, Prentice-Hall.
     1978.

539. Gordon, G. J., *Public Administration in America*, New York,
     St. Martin's Press. 1978.

540. Lorch, R. S., *Public Administration*, St. Paul, MN, West.
     1978.

541. Miewald, R., *Public Administration*, New York, McGraw-Hill.
     1978.

542. Peters, B. G., *The Politics of Bureaucracy*, New York,
     Longman. 1978.

543. Shafritz, J., et al., *Personnel Management in Government*,
     New York, Dekker. 1978.

544. Sharkansky, I., (1975), Fourth Edition. 1978.

545. Walsh, A. H., *The Public's Business*, Cambridge, MA,
     M. I. T. Press. 1978.

546. Wright, D. S., *Understanding Intergovernmental Relations*,
     North Scituate, MA, Duxbury Press. 1978.

547. Anderson, J. E., (1975), Second Edition. 1979.

548. Bernstein, S. J., and O'Hara, P., *Public Administration*,
      New York, Harper and Row. 1979.

549. Bozeman, B., *Public Management and Policy Analysis*,
      New York, St. Martin's Press. 1979.

550. Fox, D. M., *Managing the Public's Interest*, New York,
      Holt, Rinehart and Winston. 1979.

551. Heady, F. C., (1966), Second Edition, New York, Dekker.
      1979.

552. Henry, N. L., (1975), Second Edition. 1979.

553. Hill, L. B., and Herbert, F. T., *Essentials of Public
      Administration*, North Scituate, MA, Duxbury Press.
      1979.

554. Lee, R. D., *Public Personnel Systems*, Baltimore, MD,
      University Park Press. 1979.

555. Lutrin, C. F., and Settle, A. K., (1976), Second Edition.
      1979.

556. McKinney, J. B., and Howard, L. C., *Public Administration*,
      Oak Park, IL, Moore. 1979.

557. Robbins, S. P., (1976), Second Edition. 1979.

558. Wildavsky, A., (1974), Third Edition. 1979.

559. Cayer, N. J., *Managing Human Resources*, New York,
      St. Martin's Press. 1980.

560. Choi, Y. H., *Introduction to Public Administration*,
      Virginia Beach, VA, Donning. 1980.

561. Fesler, J. W., *Public Administration: Theory and Prac-
      tice*, Englewood Cliffs, NJ, Prentice-Hall. 1980.

562. Frederickson, H. G., *New Public Administration*,
      University, AL, The University of Alabama Press. 1980.

563. Gortner, H. F., (1977), Second Edition. 1980.

564. Morrow, W. L., (1975), Second Edition. 1980.

565. Nachmias, D., and Rosenbloom, D., *Bureaucratic Government*,
      U. S. A., New York, St. Martin's Press. 1980.

566. Nigro, F. A., and Nigro, L. C., (1977), Fifth Edition.
      1980.

567. Pursley, R. D., and Shortland, M., *Managing Government
      Organizations*, North Scituate, MA, Duxbury Press. 1980.

568. Waldo, D., *The Enterprise of Public Administration*,
      Novato, CA, Chandler and Sharp. 1980.

569. Williams, J. D., *Public Administration: The People's
      Business*, Boston: Little, Brown. 1980.

570. Berkley, G. E., (1978), Third Edition. 1981.

571. Cutchin, D. A., *Guide to Public Administration*, Itasca,
      IL, Peacock. 1981.

572. Dimock, M. E., *Law and Dynamic Administration*, New York,
      Praeger. 1981.

573. Eddy, W. B., *Public Organization Behavior and Develop-
      ment*, Boston, Little, Brown. 1981.

574. Garson, E. D., and Williams, J. O., *Public Administration*,
      Boston, Allyn and Bacon. 1981.

575. Gordon, G. J., (1978), Second Edition. 1981.

576. Kramer, F. A., (1977), Second Edition. 1981.

577. Lynn, L. E., *Managing the Public's Business*, New York,
      Basic Books. 1981.

578. Nigro, F. A., and Nigro, L. C., (1976), Second Edition.
      1981.

579. Shafritz, J., et al. (1978), Second Edition. 1981.

580. Walker, D. B., *Toward a Functioning Federalism*, Cambridge,
      MA, Winthrop. 1981.

581. Anderson, J. E., (1979), Third Edition.

582. Caiden, G. E., (1971), Second Edition. Pacific Palisades,
      CA, Palisades Publishers. 1982.

583. Dimock, Dimock, and Fox, D. M., (1969), Fifth Edition.
      1982.

584. Mikesell, J. L., *Fiscal Administration*, Homewood, IL,
      Dorsey. 1982.

585. Mosher, F. C., (1968), Second Edition. 1982.

586. Sharkansky, I., *Public Administration: Agencies, Policies
      and Politics*, San Francisco, W. H. Freeman. 1982.

587. Starling, G., (1977), Second Edition. 1982.

III. GENERAL ANTHOLOGIES IN AMERICAN PUBLIC ADMINISTRATION

     The basic text is usually written by one or two persons
who undertake the arduous task of covering the field systematically. In contrast, a general anthology is a collection of
specially written pieces or articles reprinted from professional
journals. It serves different purposes. Anthologies can be
(a) convenient handbooks of the classic writings in the discipline that may be otherwise inaccessible, (b) illustrative
manuals to accompany a basic text, (c) special collections designed for experimental courses in new frontiers of the discipline, and (d) colloquia of disparate and controversial views
and approaches to the discipline. The following are considered
to be worthwhile student companions, to aid intellectual development beyond textbook descriptions and analyses.

588. Seckler-Hudson, C., ed., *Processes of Organization and
      Management*, Washington, DC, Public Affairs Press. 1948.

589. Lepawsky, A., ed., *Administration*, New York, Knopf. 1949.

590. Nigro, F. A., ed., *Public Administration*, New York,
      Holt, Rinehart and Winston. 1951.

591. Merton, R. K., et al., eds., *Reader in Bureaucracy*,
      New York, Free Press. 1951.

592. Waldo, D., ed., *Ideas and Issues in Public Administration*,
      New York, Macmillan. 1953.

593. Rowat, D. C., ed., *Basic Issues in Public Administration*,
      New York, Macmillan. 1961.

594. Mailick, S., and Van Ness, E.H., eds., *Concepts and Issues in Administrative Behavior*, Englewood Cliffs, NJ, Prentice-Hall. 1962.

595. March, J. G., ed., *A Handbook of Organizations*, Chicago, Rand McNally. 1965.

596. Martin, R. C., ed., *Public Administration and Democracy*, Syracuse, NY, Syracuse University Press. 1965.

597. Rourke, F. E., ed., *Bureaucratic Power in National Politics*, Boston, Little, Brown. 1965.

598. Bauer, R. A., ed., *Social Indicators*, Cambridge, MA, MIT Press. 1966.

599. Golembiewski, R. T., Gibson, F., Carnog, G. Y., eds., *Public Administration*, Chicago, Rand McNally. 1966.

600. Hawley, C. E., and Weintraub, R. E., ed., *Administrative Questions and Political Answers*, Princeton, NJ, Van Nostrand. 1966.

601. O'Donnell, M. E., ed., *Readings in Public Administration*, Boston, Houghton Mifflin. 1966.

602. Woll, P., ed., *Public Administration and Policy*, New York, Harper and Row. 1966.

603. Raphaeli, N., ed., *Readings in Comparative Public Administration*, Boston, Allyn and Bacon. 1967.

604. Altschuler, A. A., ed., *The Politics of the Federal Bureaucracy*, New York, Dodd, Mead. 1968.

605. Golembiewski, R. T., ed., *Public Budgeting and Finance*, Itasca, IL, Peacock. 1968.

606. Lyden, F. J., Kroll, M., Shipman, G. A., eds., *Policies, Decisions and Organizations*, New York, Appleton-Century-Crofts. 1969.

607. Lyden, F. J., and Miller, E. G., eds., *Public Budgeting: Program, Planning, and Evaluation*, Chicago, Rand McNally. 1969.

608. Reagan, M. D., ed., *The Administration of Public Policy*, Glenview, IL, Scott, Foresman. 1969.

609. Banfield, E. C., ed., *Urban Government*, New York, Free Press. 1969.

610. Bennis, W. G., ed., *American Bureaucracy*, New Brunswick, NJ, Transaction Books. 1970.

611. Gawthrop, L. C., ed., *The Administrative Process and Democratic Theory*, Boston, Houghton Mifflin. 1970.

612. Golembiewski, R. T., and Cohen, M., eds., *People in Public Service*, Itasca, IL, Peacock. 1970.

613. Brown, D. S., ed., *Federal Contributions to Management*, New York, Praeger. 1971.

614. Uveges, J. A., ed., *The Dimensions of Public Administration*, Boston, Holbrook. 1971.

615. Yarwood, D. L., ed., *The National Administrative System*, New York, Wiley. 1971.

616. Golembiewski, R. T., Gibson, and Carnog, eds. (1966), Second Edition. 1971.

617. Rourke, F. E., ed. (1965), Second Edition. 1971.

618. Feld, R. D., and Grafton, C., eds., *The Uneasy Partnership*, Palo Alto, CA, National Press. 1973.

619. Hills, G. W., et al., eds., *Conducting the Public's Business*, Norman, University of Oklahoma Press. 1973.

620. Kramer, F. A., ed., *Perspectives on Public Bureaucracy*, Cambridge, MA, Winthrop. 1973.

621. Storm, B., and Jun, J. S., eds., *Tomorrow's Organizations*, Glenview, IL, Scott, Foresman and Company. 1973.

622. Dolbeare, K. M., eds., *Public Policy Evaluation*, Beverly Hills, CA, Sage Publications. 1975.

623. Golembiewski, R. T., and Rubin, J., eds. (1968), Second Edition. 1975.

624. Holden, M., and Dresang, D. L., eds., *What Government Does*, Beverly Hills, CA, Sage Publications. 1975.

625. Holzer, M., ed., *Productivity in Public Organizations*,
      Port Washington, NY, Dunellen. 1975.

626. Mosher, F. C., ed., *American Public Administration:
      Past, Present and Future*, University, AL, University
      of Alabama Press. 1975.

627. Uveges, J. A., ed. (1971), Second Edition. 1975.

628. Golembiewski, R. T., and Cohen, M., eds. (1970),
      Second Edition. 1976.

629. Golembiewski, Gibson and Carnog, eds. (1972), Third
      Edition. 1976.

630. Mosher, F. C., ed., *Basic Documents of American Public
      Administration 1776-1950*, New York, Holmes and Meier.
      1976.

631. Stillman, R. J., ed., *Public Administration*, Boston,
      Houghton Mifflin. 1976.

632. Altschuler, A. A., and Thomas, N. C., eds. (1968),
      Second Edition. 1977.

633. Fain, T. G., Plant, K. C., and Milloy, R., eds.,
      Federal Reorganization, New York, Bowker. 1977.

634. Frederickson, H. G., and Wise, C. R., eds., *Public
      Administration and Public Policy*, Lexington, MA, Lex-
      ington Books. 1977.

635. Kramer, F. A., ed. (1973), Second Edition. 1977.

636. Levine, C. H., ed., *Managing Human Resources*, Beverly
      Hills, CA, Sage Publications. 1977.

637. Lane, F. S., ed., *Current Issues in Public Administra-
      tion*, New York, St. Martin's Press. 1978.

638. Rourke, F. E., ed. (1972), Third Edition. 1978.

639. Shafritz, J. M., and Hyde, A. C., eds., *Classics of
      Public Administration*, Oak Park, IL, Moore. 1978.

640. Sutherland, J. W., ed., *Management Handbook for Public
      Administration*, New York, Van Nostrand Reinhold. 1978.

641. Hyde, A. C., and Shafritz, J. M., eds., *Program Evaluation in the Public Sector*, New York, Praeger. 1979.

642. Kramer, F. A., ed., *Contemporary Approaches to Public Budgeting*, Cambridge, MA, Winthrop. 1979.

643. Lowi, T. J., and Stone, A., eds., *Nationalizing Government*, Beverly Hills, CA, Sage Publications. 1979.

644. May, J. V., and Wildavsky, A. B., eds., *The Policy Cycle*, Beverly Hills, CA, Sage Publications. 1979.

645. Sarri, R. C., and Hasenfeld, Y., eds., *Management of Human Services*, New York, Columbia University Press. 1979.

646. Thompson, F. J., ed., *Classics of Public Personnel Policy*, Oak Park, IL, Moore. 1979.

647. Uveges, J. A., ed. (1975), Third Edition. 1979.

648. Bellone, C. J., ed., *Organization Theory and the New Public Administration*, Boston, Allyn and Bacon. 1980.

649. Klinger, D. E., ed., *Public Personnel Management*, Englewood Cliffs, NJ, Prentice-Hall. 1980.

650. Lane, F. S., ed., *Managing State and Local Government*. New York, St. Martin's Press. 1980.

651. Levine, C. H., ed., *Managing Fiscal Stress*, Chatham, NY, Chatham House. 1980.

652. Levine, C. H., and Rubin, I., eds., *Fiscal Stress and Public Policy*, Beverly Hills, CA, Sage Publications. 1980.

653. Newland, C. A., ed., *Professional Public Executives*, Washington, DC, American Society for Public Administration. 1980.

654. Orlans, H., ed., *Nonprofit Organizations*, New York, Praeger. 1980.

655. Peterson, J. E., and Spain, C. L., eds., *Essays in Public Finance and Financial Management*, Chatham, NY, Chatham House. 1980.

656. Schick, A., ed., *Perspectives on Budgeting*, Washington,
      DC, American Society for Public Administration. 1980.

657. Siegel, G. B., ed., *Breaking with Orthodoxy in Public
      Administration*, Washington, DC, University Press of
      America, Inc. 1980.

658. Stillman, R. J., ed. (1976), Second Edition. 1980.

659. Weiss, C. H., and Barton, A. H., eds., *Making Bureau-
      cracies Work*, Beverly Hills, CA, Sage Publications.
      1980.

660. White, M. J., et al., eds., *Managing Public Systems*,
      North Scituate, MA, Duxbury Press. 1980.

661. Golembiewski, R. T., ed., *Approaches to Organizing*,
      Washington, DC, American Society for Public Administra-
      tion. 1980.

662. Kim, J. T., ed., *New Readings in American Public
      Administration*, Dubuque, ID, Kendall/Hunt. 1980.

663. Kramer, F. A., ed. (1977), Third Edition. 1980.

664. Mosher, F. C., ed., *Basic Literature of American Public
      Administration, 1787-1950*, New York, Holmes and Meier.
      1980.

665. Murphy, T. P., et al., eds., *Contemporary Public
      Administration*, Itasca, IL, Peacock. 1980.

666. Vocino, T., and Rabin, J., eds., *Contemporary Public
      Administration*, New York, Harcourt Brace Jovanovich.
      1980.

667. Horton, F. W., and Marchand, D. A., eds., *Information
      Management in Public Administration*, Arlington, VA,
      Information Resources Press. 1982.

668. Lane, F. S., ed. (1978), Second Edition. 1982.

669. Perry, J. L., and Kraemer, K. L., ed., *Public Manage-
      ment: Public and Private Perspectives*, Palo Alto,
      CA, Mayfield. 1982.

670. Uveges, J. A., ed., *Public Administration*, New York,
      Dekker. 1982.

IV. BIBLIOGRAPHIES, CASE STUDIES AND WORKBOOKS IN AMERICAN
     PUBLIC ADMINISTRATION

     Case studies are designed to give students a feel of
actual practice and to acquaint those without any personal
experience or knowledge in public administration with the public official's world. They may take them through a complete
episode or present a suggestive scenario to be acted out in
different roles. At one time, cases were believed to constitute the new educational wave, but they have not been used as
widely as in other professional fields. All make engrossing
reading. Explanations of the use of case studies usually
introduce each book. Recent resource books are also cited here.

671. Stein, H., *Public Administration and Policy Development*,
      New York, Harcourt, Brace. 1952.

672. Redford, E. S., *Public Administration and Policy Forma-
      tion*, Austin, University of Texas Press. 1956.

673. Bock, E. A., *Essays on the Case Method in Public Adminis-
      tration*, Syracuse, NY, Inter-University Case Program,
      Inc., Syracuse University. 1962.

674. Bock, E. A., *State and Local Government*, University,
      AL, University of Alabama Press. 1963.

675. Stein, H., *American Civil Military Decisions*, University,
      AL, University of Alabama Press. 1963.

676. Mosher, F. C., *Governmental Reorganizations*, Indianapolis,
      Bobbs-Merrill. 1967.

677. Golembiewski, R. T., *Perspectives on Public Management*,
      Itasca, IL, Peacock. 1968.

678. Nash, G. D., *Perspectives on Administration*, Berkeley,
      CA, Institute of Governmental Studies. 1969.

679. Novogrod, J., Dimock, E. O., and Dimock, M. E., *Casebook
      in Public Administration*, New York, Holt, Rinehart and
      Winston. 1969.

680.   Golembiewski, R. T., *Cases in Public Management*, Chicago, Rand McNally. 1973.

681.   McCurdy, H. E., *Public Administration: A Bibliography*, Washington, DC, The American University. 1973.

682.   Byrd, J., *Operations Research Models for Public Administration*, Lexington, MA, Lexington Books. 1975.

683.   Anderson, J. E., *Cases in Public Policy Management*, New York, Praeger. 1976.

684.   Golembiewski, R. T., (1968), Second Edition. 1976.

685.   Golembiewski, R. T., and White, M., (1973), Second Edition. 1976.

686.   Simpson, A. E., *Guide to Library Research in Public Administration*, New York, John Jay College of Criminal Justice. 1976.

687.   Palic, V. M., *Government Publication*, New York, Pergamon. 1977.

688.   Henry, N. L., *Doing Public Administration*, Boston, MA, Allyn and Bacon. 1978.

689.   Present, P. E., *People and Public Administration*, Pacific Palisades, CA, Palisades Publishers. 1979.

690.   Uveges, J. A., *Cases in Public Administration*, Boston, MA, Holbrook. 1979.

691.   Briscoe, D. R., and Leonardson, G. S., *Experiences in Public Administration*, North Scituate, MA, Duxbury Press. 1980.

692.   Golembiewski and White (1976), Third Edition. 1980.

693.   Lynn, L. E., *Designing Public Policy*, Santa Monica, CA, Goodyear. 1980.

694.   Matlack, W. F., *Statistics for Public Policy and Management*, Belmont, MA, Duxbury Press. 1980.

695.   Meier, K. J., and Brudney, J. L., *Applied Statistics for Public Administration*, Monterey, CA, Duxbury Press. 1980.

696. Murphy, J. T., *Getting the Facts*, Santa Monica, CA, Goodyear. 1980.

697. Rouse, J. E., *Public Administration in American Society*, Detroit, Gale Research Co. 1980.

698. Allan, P. and Rosenberg, S., *Public Personnel and Administrative Behavior*, Monterey, CA, Duxbury Press. 1981.

699. Chandler, R. C., and Plano, J. C., *The Public Administration Dictionary*, New York, Wiley. 1981.

700. Holzer, M., and Rosen, E. D., *Current Cases in Public Administration*, Monterey, CA, Duxbury Press. 1981.

701. Murin, W. J., et al., *Public Policy: A Guide to Information Sources*, Detroit, MI, Gale Research Co. 1982.

702. Bingham, R. D., and Ethridge, M. E., *Reaching Decisions in Public Policy and Administration*, New York, Longman. 1982.

703. Bresnick, D. A., *Public Organizations and Policy*, Glenview, IL, Scott, Foresman. 1982.

704. Rosenthal, S. R., *Managing Government Operations*, Glenview, IL, Scott, Foresman. 1982.

705. Welch, S., and Comer, J., *Quantitative Methods for Public Administration*, Homewood, IL, Dorsey. 1982.

V. FREQUENTLY CITED CONTEMPORARY TEXTS

Several contemporary texts published since 1960 have become classics in their own time as attested by the frequency with which they are (a) reissued, (b) cited by other authorities, and (c) required or recommended as reading by over two hundred university programs and the National Association of Schools of Public Affairs and Administration. As it takes time for a new work to become known and widely read, there is some lag between the publication date and extensive use. For this reason, the following list tends to under-emphasize books published since 1975. It is derived from the Social Science Citation Index, a sample of NASPAA programs, and correlation among current bibliographies and guides in public administration. It excludes core texts, general anthologies, and case studies.

706.   Aaron, H. J., *Politics and Professors*, Washington, DC, Brookings, 1978.

707.   Alinsky, S. D., *Rules for Radicals*, New York, Random House, 1971.

708.   Allen, T. H., *New Methods in Social Science Research: Policy Sciences and Futures Research*, New York, Praeger, 1978.

709.   Allison, G. T., *Essence of Decision*, Boston, Little, Brown, 1971.

710.   Altschuler, A. A., *Community Control*, New York, Pegasus, 1970.

711.   Anton, T. J., *The Politics of State Expenditures in Illinois*, Urbana, University of Illinois Press, 1966.

712.   Argyris, C., *Interpersonal Competence and Organizational Effectiveness*, Homewood, IL, Irwin, 1962.

713.   Argyris, C., *Integrating the Individual and the Organization*, New York, Wiley, 1964.

714.   Arrow, K. J., *The Limits of Organizations*, New York, Norton, 1974.

715.   Banfield, E. C., *The Unheavenly City*, Boston, Little, Brown, 1968.

716.   Bardach, E., *The Implementation Game*, Cambridge, MA, MIT Press, 1977.

717.   Bauer, R. A., and Gergen, K. J., eds., *The Study of Policy Formulation*, New York, The Free Press, 1968.

718.   Bennis, W. G., *Changing Organizations*, New York, McGraw-Hill, 1966.

719.   Bennis, W. G., *Organization Development*, Reading, MA, Addison-Wesley, 1969.

720.   Bennis, W. G., et al., eds., *The Planning of Change*, New York, Holt, Rinehart and Winston, 1961.

721.   Bennis, W. G., and Slater, P. E., *The Temporary Society*, New York, Harper and Row, 1968.

722. Berkley, G. E., *The Administrative Revolution*, Englewood Cliffs, NJ, Prentice-Hall, 1971.

723. Berman, L., *The Office of Management and Budget and the Presidency 1921-1979*, Princeton, NJ, Princeton University Press, 1979.

724. Blau, P. M., and Scott, W. R., *Formal Organizations*, San Francisco, Chandler, 1962.

725. Bok, S., *Lying*, New York, Pantheon Books, 1978.

726. Braybrooke, D., and Lindblom, C., *A Strategy of Decision*, New York, Free Press of Glencoe, 1963.

727. Buchanan, J. M., and Tullock, G., *The Calculus of Consent*, Ann Arbor, MI, University of Michigan Press, 1962.

728. Caiden, G. E., *Administrative Reform*, Chicago, Aldine, 1969.

729. Caiden, N. J., and Wildavsky, A., *Planning and Budgeting in Poor Countries*, New York, Wiley, 1974.

730. Caldwell, L. K., *Man and His Environment: Policy and Administration*, New York, Harper and Row, 1975.

731. Caputo, D. A., and Cole, R. L., eds., *Revenue Sharing: Methodological Approaches and Problems*, Lexington, MA, Lexington Books, 1976.

732. Caro, R. A., *The Power Broker*, New York, Knopf, 1974.

733. Cleveland, H., *The Future Executive*, New York, Harper and Row, 1972.

734. Corson, J. J., and Shale, P. R., *Men Near the Top*, Baltimore, The Johns Hopkins Press, 1966.

735. Crane, E., et al., *State Government Productivity*, New York, Praeger, 1976.

736. Crecine, J. P., *Governmental Problem-Solving: A Computer Simulation of Municipal Budgeting*, Chicago, Rand McNally, 1969.

737. Cyert, R. M., and March, J. G., *A Behavioral Theory of the Firm*, Englewood Cliffs, NJ, Prentice-Hall, 1963.

738. Dahl, R. A., *Who Governs?*, New Haven, CT, Yale University Press, 1961.

739. Danhof, C. H., *Government Contracting and Technological Change*, Washington, DC, Brookings, 1967.

740. Dodd, L. C., and Schott, R. L., *Congress and the Administrative State*, New York, Wiley, 1979.

741. Downs, A., *Inside Bureaucracy*, Boston, MA, Little, Brown, 1967.

742. Dvorin, E. P., and Simmons, R. H., *From Amoral to Humane Bureaucracy*, San Francisco, CA, Canfield Press, 1972.

743. Eichner, A. S., and Brecher, C. M., *Controlling Social Expenditures*, New York, Universe Books, 1979.

744. Elazar, D. J., *American Federalism*, New York, Crowell, 1966.

745. Etzioni, A., *Modern Organizations*, Englewood Cliffs, NJ, Prentice-Hall, 1964.

746. Etzioni, A., *A Comparative Analysis of Complex Organizations*, New York, Free Press, 1975.

747. Fenno, R. F., *The Power of the Purse*, Boston, MA, Little, Brown, 1966.

748. Fitzgerald, A. E., *High Priests of Waste*, New York, Norton, 1972.

749. Fleishman, J. L., ed., *Public Duties*, Cambridge, MA, Harvard University Press, 1981.

750. Friedman, L. B., *Budgeting Municipal Expenditures*, New York, Praeger, 1975.

751. Fritschler, A. L., *Smoking and Politics*, Englewood Cliffs, NJ, Prentice-Hall, 1975.

752. Fromm, G., ed., *Studies in Public Regulation*, Cambridge, MA, MIT Press, 1981.

753. Gable, R. W., and Springer, J. F., *Administering Agricultural Development in Asia*, Boulder, CO, Westview Press, 1976.

754. Galbraith, J. K., *The New Industrial State*, Boston, MA, Houghton Mifflin, 1967.

755. Gates, B. L., *Social Program Administration*, Englewood Cliffs, NJ, Prentice-Hall, 1980.

756. Gawthrop, L. C., *Bureaucratic Behavior in the Executive Branch*, New York, Free Press, 1969.

757. Gawthrop, L. C., *The Administrative Process and Democratic Theory*, Boston, MA, Houghton Mifflin, 1970.

758. Gellhorn, W., *When Americans Complain*, Cambridge, MA, Harvard University Press, 1966.

759. Golembiewski, R. T., *Renewing Organizations*, Itasca, IL, Peacock, 1972.

760. Gore, W. J., *Administrative Decision Making*, New York, Wiley, 1964.

761. Graves, W. B., *American Intergovernmental Relations*, New York, Scribner, 1964.

762. Gross, B. M., *The Managing of Organizations*, New York, Free Press, 1964.

763. Gross, B. M., *Friendly Fascism*, New York, M. Evans, 1980.

764. Hallman, H., *Administrative Decentralization and Citizen Control*, Washington, DC, Center for Governmental Studies, 1971.

765. Harris, J. P., *Congressional Control of Administration*, Washington, DC, Brookings, 1964.

766. Hatry, H. P., et al., *Program Analysis for State and Local Government*, Washington, DC, The Urban Institute, 1973.

767. Haveman, R. H., and Margolis, J., eds., *Public Expenditures and Policy Analysis*, Chicago, IL, Rand McNally, 1970.

768. Hawley, W. D., and Rogers, D., eds., *Improving the Quality of Urban Management*, Beverly Hills, CA, Sage Publications, 1974.

769.   Heclo, H., *A Government of Strangers*, Washington, DC,
       Brookings, 1977.

770.   Heclo, H., and Salamon, L. M., eds., *The Illusion of
       Presidential Government*, Boulder, CO, Westview, 1981.

771.   Hess, S., *Organizing the Presidency*, Washington, DC,
       Brookings, 1976.

772.   Hirsch, F., *Social Limits to Growth*, Cambridge, MA,
       Harvard University Press, 1976.

773.   Hoos, I. R., *Systems Analysis in Public Policy*,
       Berkeley, CA, University of California Press, 1972.

774.   Howard, S. K., *Changing State Budgeting*, Lexington,
       KY, Council of State Governments, 1973.

775.   Hubbell, L. K., ed., *Fiscal Crisis in American Cities:
       The Federal Response*, Cambridge, MA, Ballinger, 1979.

776.   Hummel, R. P., *The Bureaucratic Experience*, New York,
       St. Martin's Press, 1977.

777.   Ippolito, D. S., *The Budget and National Politics*,
       San Francisco, CA, Freeman, 1978.

778.   Jacoby, H., *The Bureaucratization of the World*,
       Berkeley, CA, University of California Press, 1976.

779.   Kahn, R. L., et al., *Organizational Stress*, New York,
       Wiley, 1965.

780.   Katz, D., and Kahn, R. L., *The Social Psychology of
       Organizations*, New York, Wiley, 1966.

781.   Kaufman, H., *The Limits of Organizational Change*,
       University, AL, University of Alabama Press, 1971.

782.   Kaufman, H., *Are Government Organizations Immortal?*,
       Washington, DC, Brookings, 1976.

783.   Kaufman, H., *Red Tape*, Washington, DC, Brookings, 1977.

784.   Kharasch, R. N., *The Institutional Imperative*, New York,
       Charterhouse Books, 1973.

785. Kilpatrick, F. P., et al., *The Image of Federal Service*, Washington, DC, Brookings, 1964.

786. Kimberly, J. R., et al., *The Organizational Life Cycle*, San Francisco, CA, Jossey-Bass, 1980.

787. Kramer, R. M., *Voluntary Agencies in the Welfare State*, Berkeley, CA, University of California Press, 1981.

788. Kransnow, E. G., and Langley, L. D., *The Politics of Broadcasting Regulation*, New York, St. Martin's Press, 1973.

789. Krantz, H., *The Participatory Bureaucracy*, Lexington, MA, Lexington Books, 1976.

790. Krislov, S., *Representative Bureaucracy*, Englewood Cliffs, NJ, Prentice-Hall, 1974.

791. La Palombara, J., ed., *Bureaucracy and Political Development*, Princeton, NJ, Princeton University Press, 1963.

792. Lawrence, P. R., and Lorsch, J. W., *Organization and Environment*, Homewood, IL, Irwin, 1969.

793. Lee, R. D., and Johnson, R. W., *Public Budgeting Systems*, Baltimore, MD, University Park Press, 1979.

794. Levine, R. A., *Public Planning: Failure and Redirection*, New York, Basic Books, 1972.

795. Lewis, E., *Public Entrepreneurship*, Bloomington, IN, Indiana University Press, 1980.

796. Likert, R., *New Patterns of Management*, New York, McGraw-Hill, 1961.

797. Likert, R., *The Human Organization*, New York, McGraw-Hill, 1967.

798. Lindblom, C. E., *The Intelligence of Democracy*, New York, Free Press, 1964.

799. Lindblom, C. E., *The Policy Making Process*, Englewood Cliffs, NJ, Prentice-Hall, 1968.

800. Lipsky, M., *Street Level Bureaucracy*, New York, Russell Sage, 1980.

801. Lowi, T. J., *The End of Liberalism*, New York, Norton, 1969.

802. Lynn, L. E., *The State and Human Services*, Cambridge, MA, MIT Press, 1980.

803. McConnell, G., *Private Power and American Democracy*, New York, Knopf, 1966.

804. Mainzer, L. C., *Political Bureaucracy*, Glenview, IL, Scott, Foresman and Company, 1973.

805. Majone, G., and Quade, E. S., eds., *Pitfalls of Analysis*, New York, Wiley, 1980.

806. Marris, P., and Rein, M., *Dilemmas of Social Reform*, New York, Atherton, 1969.

807. Meltsner, A., *Policy Analysts in the Bureaucracy*, Berkeley, CA, University of California Press, 1976.

808. Meyer, M. W., *Change in Public Bureaucracies*, New York, Cambridge University Press, 1979.

809. Morgan, D. R., *Managing Urban America*, North Scituate, MA, Duxbury Press, 1979.

810. Mosher, F. C., *Governmental Reorganizations*, Indianapolis, IN, Bobbs-Merrill, 1967.

811. Mosher, F. C., *The GAO*, Boulder, CO, Westview Press, 1979.

812. Mosher, F. C., et al., *Watergate: Implications for Responsive Government*, New York, Basic Books, 1974.

813. Moynihan, D. P., *Maximum Feasible Misunderstanding*, New York, Free Press, 1968.

814. Musgrave, R. A., and Musgrave, P. E., *Public Finance in Theory and Practice*, New York, McGraw-Hill, 1973.

815. Nader, R., Petkas, P., and Blackwell, K., eds., *Whistle Blowing*, New York, Bantam, 1972.

816. Nakamura, R. T., and Smallwood, F., *The Politics of Policy Implementation*, New York, St. Martin's Press, 1980.

817. Nathan, R. P., *The Plot that Failed*, New York, Wiley, 1975.

818. Netzer, D., *The Subsidized Muse*, New York, Cambridge University Press, 1978.

819. Nielsen, W. A., *The Endangered Sector*, New York, Columbia University Press, 1979.

820. Niskanen, W. A., *Bureaucracy and Representative Government*, Chicago, IL, Aldine, 1971.

821. Novick, D., ed., *Program Budgeting*, Cambridge, MA, Harvard University Press, 1965.

822. Nystroom, P. C., and Starbuck, W. H., eds., *Handbook of Organizational Design*, New York, Oxford University Press, 1981.

823. O'Connor, J., *The Fiscal Crisis of the State*, New York, St. Martin's Press, 1973.

824. Okun, A. M., *Equality and Efficiency*, Washington, DC, Brookings, 1975.

825. Olson, M., *The Logic of Collective Action*, Cambridge, MA, Harvard University Press, 1965.

826. Pechman, J. A., *Federal Tax Policy*, Washington, DC, Brookings, 1966.

827. Piven, F. F., and Cloward, R. A., *Regulating the Poor*, New York, Random House, 1971.

828. Pressman, J. L., and Wildavsky, A., *Implementation*, Berkeley, CA, University of California Press, 1973.

829. Presthus, R. V., *The Organizational Society*, New York, Vintage Books, 1962.

830. Pyhrr, P. A., *Zero Base Budgeting*, New York, Wiley, 1973.

831. Quade, E. S., *Analysis for Public Decisions*, New York, Elsevier, 1975.

832. Reagan, M. D., *The Managed Economy*, New York, Wiley, 1963.

833. Reagan, M. D., *The New Federalism*, New York, Oxford
      University Press, 1972.

834. Redford, E. S., *Democracy in the Administrative State*,
      New York, Oxford University Press, 1969.

835. Rhoads, S. E., ed., *Valuing Life: Public Policy
      Dilemmas*, Boulder, CO, Westview, 1980.

836. Riggs, F. W., *Administration in Developing Countries*,
      Boston, Houghton Mifflin, 1964.

837. Riggs, F. W., ed., *Frontiers of Development Administra-
      tion*, Durham, NC, Duke University Press, 1971.

838. Ripley, R. B., and Franklin, G. A., *Congress, The
      Bureaucracy and Public Policy*, Homewood, IL, Dorsey
      Press, 1976.

839. Rivlin, A. M., *Systematic Thinking for Social Action*,
      Washington, DC, Brookings, 1971.

840. Rogers, D., *110 Livingston St.*, New York, Random House,
      1969.

841. Rohr, J. A., *Ethics for Bureaucrats*, New York, Marcel
      Dekker, 1978.

842. Rose, R., *Managing Presidential Objectives*, New York,
      Free Press, 1976.

843. Rosenbloom, D. H., *Federal Service and the Constitution*,
      Ithaca, NY, Cornell University Press, 1971.

844. Rourke, F. E., *Secrecy and Publicity*, Baltimore, MD,
      The Johns Hopkins University Press, 1961.

845. Rourke, F. E., *Bureaucracy, Politics and Public Policy*,
      Boston, MA, Little, Brown, 1969.

846. Sapolsky, H. M., *The Polaris System Development*, Cam-
      bridge, MA, Harvard University Press, 1972.

847. Schein, E. H., *Organizational Psychology*, Englewood
      Cliffs, NJ, Prentice-Hall, 1965.

848. Schick, A., *Budget Innovation in the States*, Washington,
      DC, Brookings, 1971.

849. Schick, A., *Congress and Money*, Washington, DC, Urban Institute, 1980.

850. Schon, D., *Beyond the Stable State*, New York, Random House, 1971.

851. Schultze, C. L., *The Politics and Economics of Public Spending*, Washington, DC, Brookings, 1968.

852. Schultze, C. L., *The Public Use of Private Interest*, Washington, DC, Brookings, 1977.

853. Scott, W. G., and Hart, D. K., *Organizational America*, Boston, MA, Houghton Mifflin, 1979.

854. Seidman, H., *Politics, Position and Power*, New York, Oxford University Press, 1970.

855. Seitz, S. T., *Bureaucracy, Policy and the Public*, St. Louis, MO, Mosby, 1978.

856. Sharkansky, I., *The Politics of Taxing and Spending*, Indianapolis, IN, Bobbs-Merrill, 1969.

857. Sherman, H., *It All Depends*, University, AL, University of Alabama Press, 1966.

858. Smith, B. L. R., ed., *The Dilemma of Accountability in Modern Government*, New York, St. Martin's Press, 1971.

859. Sonenblum, S., Reis, J. S., and Kirlin, J. J., *How Cities Provide Services*, Cambridge, MA, Ballinger, 1977.

860. Spiro, H. J., *Responsibility in Government: Theory and Practice*, New York, Van Nostrand Reinhold, 1969.

861. Stanley, D. T., *The Higher Civil Service*, Washington, DC, Brookings, 1964.

862. Stone, A., *Economic Regulation and the Public Interest*, Ithaca, NY, Cornell University Press, 1977.

863. Sundquist, J. L., *Making Federalism Work*, Washington, DC, Brookings, 1969.

864. Thayer, F. C., *An End to Hierarchy! An End to Competition!*, New York, Franklin Watts, 1973.

865. Thompson, F. J., *Health Policy and the Bureaucracy*, Cambridge, MA, MIT Press, 1981.

866. Thompson, J. D., *Organization in Action*, New York, McGraw-Hill, 1967.

867. Thompson, V. A., *Modern Organization*, New York, Knopf, 1961.

868. Thompson, V. A., *Bureaucracy and Innovation*, University, AL, University of Alabama Press, 1969.

869. Thompson, V. A., *Without Sympathy or Enthusiasm*, University, AL, University of Alabama Press, 1975.

870. Tullock, G., *The Politics of Bureaucracy*, Washington, DC, Public Affairs Press, 1965.

871. Vroom, V. H., *Work and Motivation*, New York, Wiley, 1964.

872. Vroom, V. H., *Methods of Organizational Research*, Pittsburgh, PA, University of Pittsburgh Press, 1967.

873. Wamsley, G. L., and Zald, M. N., *The Political Economy of Public Organizations*, Lexington, MA, D. C. Heath, 1973.

874. Warwick, D. P., *A Theory of Public Bureaucracy*, Cambridge, MA, Harvard University Press, 1975.

875. Waterston, A., *Development Planning*, Baltimore, MD, The Johns Hopkins University Press, 1965.

876. Weidenbaum, M. L., *The Modern Public Sector*, New York, Basic Books, 1969.

877. Weiss, C. H., *Evaluation Research*, Englewood Cliffs, NJ, Prentice-Hall, 1972.

878. Wholey, J. S., et al., *Federal Evaluation Policy*, Washington, DC, Urban Institute, 1970.

879. Wildavsky, A., *Speaking Truth to Power*, Boston, MA, Little, Brown, 1979.

880. Wildavsky, A., *How to Limit Government Spending*, Berkeley, CA, University of California Press, 1980.

881. Wilensky, H. L., *Organizational Intelligence*, New York, Basic Books, 1967.

882. Wolanin, T. R., *Presidential Advisory Commissions*, Madison, WI, University of Wisconsin Press, 1975.

883. Woll, P., *Administrative Law: The Informal Process*, Berkeley, CA, University of California Press, 1963.

884. Woll, P., *American Bureaucracy*, New York, Norton, 1973.

885. Yates, D., *Bureaucratic Democracy*, Cambridge, MA, Harvard University Press, 1982.

VI. SPECIALIZED BIBLIOGRAPHIES

The volume of literature on public administration expands at such a rate that no single person can keep track of it. One is forced to be selective. It is enough for most purposes to concentrate on the major sources and most frequently cited references and to rely on specialists for specific areas. An attempt to provide a general overview of the subject was made in the bibliographical guide in G. E. Caiden, *The Dynamics of Public Administration* (New York, Holt, Rinehart and Winston, 1971) but since then the area covered by public administration has further grown and fragmented. A similar attempt today would require three times the length just to deal with the bibliographical highlights of the 1970's. Rather than repeat the exercise, a series of supplemental, specialized bibliographies, concentrating on new literature since 1965 is provided. As previously mentioned in Chapter 1, some specialties, such as criminal justice administration, administrative and public law, social work, librarianship, public health, police administration, and military administration are so self-contained and independently organized that they have been omitted from this bibliography; Chapter 2, however, should be consulted to gain access to these fields.

A. Administration and Society

These sources relate American public administration to its changing environment.

886. Bell, D., *The Coming of Post Industrial Society*, New York, Basic Books, 1973.

887. Boucher, W. I., ed., *The Study of the Future*,
      Washington, DC, National Science Foundation, 1977.

888. Ehrlich, P. R., *The End of Affluence*, New York, Ballan-
      tine, 1974.

889. Eimicke, W. B., *Public Administration in a Democratic
      Context*, Beverly Hills, CA, Sage Publications, 1974.

890. Etzioni, A., *The Active Society*, New York, Free Press,
      1968.

891. Ferkiss, V. C., *Technological Man*, New York, George
      Braziller, 1969.

892. Gardner, J. W., *In Common Cause*, New York, Norton,
      1977.

893. Gartner, A., and Reissman, F., *The Emerging Service
      Society*, New York, Harper and Row, 1974.

894. Goodsell, C. T., ed., *The Public Encounter*, Blooming-
      ton, IN, Indiana University Press, 1981.

895. Haberstam, D., *The Best and the Brightest*, New York,
      Random House, 1972.

896. Heilbroner, R. L., *An Inquiry into the Human Prospect*,
      New York, Norton, 1974.

897. Held, V., *The Public Interest and Individual Interests*,
      New York, Basic Books, 1970.

898. Janowitz, M., *The Last Half Century*, Chicago, IL,
      University of Chicago Press, 1978.

899. Lambright, W. H., *Governing Science and Technology*,
      New York, Oxford University Press, 1976.

900. Landau, M., *Political Theory and Political Science*,
      New York, Macmillan, 1972.

901. Lieberman, J. K., *The Tyranny of Experts*, New York,
      Walker, 1970.

902. Lindblom, C., *Politics and Markets*, New York, Basic
      Books, 1977.

903. Milgram, S., *Obedience to Authority*, New York, Harper and Row, 1973.

904. Pennock, J., and Chapman, J. W., *Privacy*, New York, Atherton, 1967.

905. Rawls, J., *A Theory of Justice*, Cambridge, MA, Harvard University Press, 1971.

906. Rees, J., *Equality*, New York, Praeger, 1971.

907. Reich, C. A., *The Greening of America*, New York, Random House, 1970.

908. Roszak, T., *The Making of a Counter Culture*, Garden City, NY, Anchor Books, 1969.

909. Siegan, B. H., ed., *Government, Regulation and the Economy*, Lexington, MA, Lexington Books, 1980.

910. Toffler, A., *Culture Shock*, New York, Random House, 1970.

B.   Administrative Ethics and Behavior

Watergate obviously increased concern for how public officials should conduct themselves, but even before then interest existed in the dysfunctions and bureaupathologies of public bureaucracy.

911. Amick, G., *The American Way of Graft*, Princeton, NJ, Center for the Analysis of Public Issues, 1976.

912. Beauchamp, T. L., *Ethics and Public Policy*, Englewood Cliffs, NJ, Prentice-Hall, 1975.

913. Benson, G. C., *Political Corruption in America*, Lexington, MA, Lexington Books, 1978.

914. Berg, L., et al., *Corruption in the American Political System*, Morristown, NJ, General Learning Press, 1976.

915. Cohen, R., and Witcover, J., *A Heartbeat Away*, New York, Viking Press, 1974.

916. Cooper, T. L., *The Responsible Administrator*, Port Washington, NY, Kennikat Press, 1982.

917. Cressey, D., *Theft of the Nation*, New York, Harper and Row, 1969.

918. Friedrich, C. J., *The Pathology of Politics*, New York, Harper and Row, 1972.

919. Gardiner, J. A., and Lyman, T. R., *Decisions for Sale*, New York, Praeger, 1978.

920. Gardiner, J. A., and Olson, D., *Theft of the City*, Bloomington, IN, Indiana University Press, 1974.

921. Geis, G., ed., *White Collar Criminal*, New York, Atherton Press, 1968.

922. Halperin, M. A., *Bureaucratic Politics and Foreign Policy*, Washington, DC, Brookings, 1974.

923. Kaufman, H., *The Administrative Behavior of Federal Bureau Chiefs*, Washington, DC, Brookings Institution, 1981.

924. Lasky, M., *It Didn't Start With Watergate*, New York, Dial Press, 1977.

925. Lieberman, J. K., *How the Government Breaks the Law*, New York, Stein and Day, 1972.

926. Payne, R., *The Corrupt Society*, New York, Praeger, 1975.

927. Pearson, D., and Anderson, J., *The Case Against Congress*, New York, Simon and Schuster, 1968.

928. Peters, C., and Branch, T., *Blowing the Whistle*, New York, Praeger, 1972.

929. Rose-Ackerman, S., *Corruption*, New York, Academic Press, 1978.

930. Weisband, E., and Franck, T., *Resignation in Protest*, New York, Grossman, 1975.

931. Wise, D., *The Politics of Lying*, New York, Random House, 1973.

C. American Government

Public administration shapes and is shaped by changes in the machinery of government and shifts in the balance of political power. These books address such issues.

932. Anderson, S. V., ed., *Ombudsman for American Government*, Englewood Cliffs, NJ, Prentice-Hall, 1968.

933. Arnold, R. D., *Congress and the Bureaucracy*, New Haven, CT, Yale University Press, 1979.

934. Balutis, A. P., and Heaphey, J. J., *Public Administration and the Legislative Process*, Beverly Hills, CA, Sage Publications, 1974.

935. Barker, J. D., *The Presidential Character*, Englewood Cliffs, NJ, Prentice-Hall, 1977.

936. Berger, G., *Government by Judiciary*, Cambridge, MA, Harvard University Press, 1977.

937. Berger, R., *Executive Privilege*, Cambridge, MA, Harvard University Press, 1977.

938. Crane, E., Levitz, B. F., and Shafritz, J. M., *State Government Productivity*, New York, Praeger, 1976.

939. Derthick, M., *Between State and Nation*, Washington, DC, Brookings, 1974.

940. Fain, T. G., et al., eds., *Federal Reorganization: The Executive Branch*, New York, Bowker, 1977.

941. Fantani, M., and Gittell, M., *Decentralization: Achieving Reform*, New York, Praeger, 1973.

942. Feld, R. D., and Grafton, C., eds., *The Uneasy Partnership*, Palo Alto, CA, National Press, 1973.

943. Fowler, F. J., *Citizen Attitudes Toward Local Government Services and Taxes*, Cambridge, MA, Ballinger, 1974.

944. Frederickson, H. G., ed., *Neighborhood Control in the 1970's*, New York, Chandler, 1973.

945. Freeman, J. O., *Crisis and Legitimacy*, New York, Cambridge University Press, 1978.

946.   Frieden, B. J., and Kaplan, M., *The Politics of Neglect*,
       Cambridge, MA, MIT Press, 1975.

947.   Gilb, C. L. *Hidden Hierarchies*, New York, Harper and
       Row, 1966.

948.   Glendenning, P. N., and Reeves, N. N., *Pragmatic Federal-
       ism*, Pacific Palisades, CA, Palisades Publishers, 1977.

949.   Green, M. J., *The Other Government*, New York, Norton,
       1978.

950.   Grosenick, L. E., ed., *The Administration of the New
       Federalism*, Washington, DC, American Society for
       Public Administration, 1973.

951.   Hess, S., *Organizing the Presidency*, Washington, DC,
       Brookings, 1976.

952.   Holden, M., and Dresang, D. C., eds., *What Government
       Does*, Beverly Hills, CA, Sage, 1975.

953.   Kochen, M., and Deutsch, K. M., *Decentralization*,
       Cambridge, MA, Oelgeschlager, Gunn and Hain, 1980.

954.   Morrow, W. L., *Congressional Committees*, New York,
       Scribner, 1969.

955.   Murphy, T. P., et al., *Inside the Bureaucracy*, Boulder,
       CO, Westview Press, 1978.

956.   Ogul, M. S., *Congress Oversees the Bureaucracy*,
       Pittsburgh, PA, University of Pittsburgh Press, 1976.

957.   Passel, P., and Ross, L., *State Policies and Federal
       Programs*, New York, Praeger, 1978.

958.   Proxmire, W., *Report from Wasteland*, New York, Praeger,
       1970.

959.   Redford, E. S., and Blissert, M., *Organizing the Execu-
       tive Branch: The Johnson Presidency*, Chicago, IL,
       University of Chicago Press, 1981.

960.   Rose, R. S., *Managing Presidential Objectives*, New York,
       Free Press, 1976.

961. Ross, J., and Burkhead, J., *Productivity in the Local Government Sector*, Lexington, MA, Lexington Books, 1975.

962. Shapek, R. A., *Managing Federalism*, Charlottesville, VA, Community Collaborators, 1981.

963. Wright, J. D., *The Dissent of the Governed*, New York, Academic Press, 1976.

964. Yates, D., *Neighborhood Democracy*, Lexington, MA, Lexington Books, 1973.

965. Yin, R. K., and Yates, D., *Street Level Government*, Lexington, MA, Lexington Books, 1975.

D. American Public Administration and Management

This is not so much an "honorable mention" list as a survey of some of the most adventurous and exciting writing about current trends in the field.

966. Balk, W. L., *Improving Government Productivity*, Beverly Hills, CA, Sage, 1975.

967. Becker, S. W., and Neuhauser, D., *The Efficient Organization*, New York, Elsevier, 1975.

968. Beltrami, E. J., *Models for Public Systems Analysis*, New York, Academic Press, 1977.

969. Bollens, J. C., and Ries, J. C., *The City Manager Profession*, Chicago, IL, Public Administration Service, 1969.

970. Borst, D., and Montana, P. J., eds., *Managing Non Profit Organizations*, New York, AMACOM, 1977.

971. Brown, D. S., ed., *Federal Contributions to Management*, New York, Praeger, 1971.

972. Byrd, J., *Operations Research Models for Public Administration*, Lexington, MA, D. C. Heath, 1975.

973. Cronin, T. E., and Greenberg, S. D., eds., *The Presidential Advisory System*, New York, Harper and Row, 1969.

974. Fox, D. N., *The Politics of City and State Bureaucracy*,
      Pacific Palisades, CA, Goodyear, 1975.

975. Franklin, J. L., and Thrasher, J. H., *An Introduction
      to Program Evaluation*, New York, Wiley, 1976.

976. Hatry, H. P., et al., *How Effective Are Your Community
      Services?*, Washington, DC, Urban Institute, 1977.

977. Hinrichs, H. H., and Taylor, G. M., *Systematic Analysis*,
      Pacific Palisades, CA, Goodyear, 1972.

978. Holzer, M., ed., *Productivity in Public Organizations*,
      Port Washington, NY, Dunellen, 1975.

979. Kendrick, J. W., *Understanding Productivity*, Baltimore,
      MD, Johns Hopkins University Press, 1977.

980. Langbein, L. J., *Discovering Whether Programs Work*,
      Santa Monica, CA, Goodyear, 1980.

981. Lewis, E., *American Politics in a Bureaucratic Age:
      Citizens, Constituents, Clients and Victims*, Cambridge,
      MA, Winthrop, 1977.

982. Morrisey, G. I., *Management by Objective and Results in
      the Public Sector*, Reading, MA, Addison-Wesley, 1970.

983. Odiorne, G. S., *Management Decisions by Objectives*,
      Englewood Cliffs, NJ, Prentice-Hall, 1969.

984. Rutman, L., ed., *Evaluation Research Methods*, Beverly
      Hills, CA, Sage, 1977.

985. Savas, E. S., ed., *Alternatives of Delivering Public
      Services*, Boulder, CO, Westview Press, 1977.

986. Wholey, J. S., *Evaluation and Effective Public Manage-
      ment*, Boston, MA, Little, Brown, 1982.

E. Comparative, Development and International Administration

    Contrary to popular impression, comparative administration
is very much alive and some important and impressive research
is being produced as shown below.

987. Adelman, I., and Morris, C. T., *Economic Development
      and Social Equality in Developing Countries*, Stanford,
      CA, Stanford University Press, 1973.

988. Ashford, D. E., ed., *Comparing Public Policies*, Beverly Hills, CA, Sage, 1978.

989. Benveniste, G., *The Politics of Expertise*, Berkeley, CA, Glendessary, 1972.

990. Blase, M. G., *Institution Building: A Source Book*, Beverly Hills, CA, Sage, 1973.

991. Caiden, G. E., and Siedentopf, H., eds., *Strategies for Administrative Reform*, Lexington, MA, Lexington Books, 1982.

992. Cohen, S. S., *Modern Capitalist Planning*, Cambridge, MA, Harvard University Press, 1969.

993. Coleman, D., and Nixson, F., *Economics of Change in Less Developed Countries*, New York, Wiley, 1978.

994. Cox, R. W., and Jacobson, H. N., *The Anatomy of Influence: Decision Making in International Organizations*, New Haven, CT, Yale University Press, 1973.

995. Dogon, M., ed., *The Mandarins of Western Europe*, New York, Wiley, 1975.

996. Eaton, J. C., ed., *Institution Building and Development*, Beverly Hills, CA, Sage, 1972.

997. Esman, M. J., *Administration and Development in Malaysia*, Ithaca, NY, Cornell University Press, 1972.

998. Frank, C. R., and Webb, R. C., *Income Distribution and Growth in Less Developed Countries*, Washington, DC., Brookings, 1977.

999. Friedman, W., and Garner, J. F., eds., *Government Enterprise*, New York, Columbia University Press, 1970.

1000. Gant, G., *Development Administration*, Madison, WI, University of Wisconsin Press, 1979.

1001. Gordenker, L., *International Aid and National Decisions*, Princeton, NJ, Princeton University Press, 1976.

1002. Gould, D. J., *Bureaucratic Corruption and Underdevelopment in the Third World*, New York, Pergamon Press, 1980.

1003. Heaphy, J. J., ed., *Spatial Dimensions of Development Administration*, Durham, NC, Duke University Press, 1971.

1004. Heidenheimer, H. J., *Comparative Public Policy*, New York, St. Martin's Press, 1975.

1005. Hirschman, A. C., *Exit, Voice and Loyalty*, Cambridge, MA, Harvard University Press, 1970.

1006. Ilchman, W. F., and Uphoff, N. T., *The Political Economy of Development*, Berkeley, CA, University of California Press, 1972.

1007. Musolf, L. D., *Mixed Enterprise: A Developmental Perspective*, Lexington, MA, Lexington Books, 1972.

1008. Nachmias, D., and Rosenbloom, D. H., *Bureaucratic Culture*, New York, St., Martin's Press, 1978.

1009. Paige, J. M., *Agrarian Revolution*, New York, Free Press, 1975.

1010. Reubens, E. P., ed., *The Challenge of the New International Economic Order*, Boulder, CO, Westview Press, 1981.

1011. Riggs, F. W., ed., *Frontiers of Development Administration*, Durham, NC, Duke University Press, 1974.

1012. Rubinson, R., ed., *Dynamics of World Development*, Beverly Hills, CA, Sage, 1981.

1013. Suleiman, E. N., *Politics, Power and Bureaucracy in France*, Princeton, NJ, Princeton University Press, 1974.

1014. Swerdlow, I., *The Public Administration of Economic Development*, New York, Praeger, 1975.

1015. Szalai, A., and Petrella, R., *Cross National Comparative Survey Research*, New York, Pergamon, 1976.

1016. Thurber, C. E., and Graham, L. S., eds., *Development Administration in Latin America*, Durham, NC, Duke University Press, 1973.

1017. Uri, P., *Development Without Dependence*, New York, Praeger, 1976.

1018. Waldo, D., ed., *Temporal Dimensions of Development Administration*, Durham, NC, Duke University Press, 1970.

1019. Weidner, E. W., ed., *Development Administration in Asia*, Durham, NC, Duke University Press, 1970.

1020. Weise, T. G., *International Bureaucracy*, Lexington, MA, Lexington Books, 1975.

F. Environmental Management

Environmental issues have only come into the forefront of American public administration in the last decade, but environmental management has now carved out a special place.

1021. Ackerman, B., et al., *The Uncertain Search for Environmental Quality*, New York, Free Press, 1974.

1022. Anderson, F. R., et al., *Environmental Improvement Through Economic Incentives*, Baltimore, MD, The Johns Hopkins University Press, 1977.

1023. Barkum, M., *Disaster and the Millennium*, New Haven, CT, Yale University Press, 1975.

1024. Brown, H., *The Human Future Revisited*, New York, Norton, 1978.

1025. Brown, L. R., *The Twenty Ninth Day*, New York, Norton, 1978.

1026. Caldwell, L. K., *Environment: A Challenge for Modern Society*, Garden City, NY, Natural History Press, 1970.

1027. Cole, H. S. D., et al., *Models of Doom*, New York, Universe Books, 1973.

1028. Enloe, C. H., *The Politics of Pollution in a Comparative Perspective*, New York, McKay, 1975.

1029. Ewald, W. R., *Environment and Policy*, Bloomington, IN, Indiana University Press, 1968.

1030. Goldstein, W., ed., *Planning, Politics and Public Interest*, New York, Columbia University Press, 1978.

1031. Goodfield, J. G., *Playing God*, New York, Random House, 1977.

1032.   Grad, F. P., et al., *The Automobile*, Norman, OK,
        University of Oklahoma Press, 1975.

1033.   Hardin, G., and Baden, J., *Managing the Commons*, San
        Francisco, CA, Freeman, 1977.

1034.   Maddox, J., *The Doomsday Syndrome*, New York, McGraw-
        Hill, 1972.

1035.   Mann, D. E., ed., *Environmental Policy Implementation*,
        Lexington, MA, Lexington Books, 1982.

1036.   Meadows, D., et al., *The Limits to Growth*, New York,
        Universe Books, 1972.

1037.   Morgan, A. E., *Dams and Other Disasters*, Boston, MA,
        Porter Sargeant, 1971.

1038.   Nagel, S. S., ed., *Environmental Politics*, New York,
        Praeger, 1974.

1039.   Nordland, W. J., *Energy and Employment*, New York, Praeger,
        1980.

1040.   Ophuls, W., *Ecology and the Politics of Scarcity*, San
        Francisco, CA, Freeman, 1977.

1041.   Perelman, L. J., *The Global Mind*, New York, Mason/Charter,
        1976.

1042.   Pirages, D., and Ehrlich, P., *Ark II*, San Francisco, CA,
        Freeman, 1974.

1043.   Rosenbaum, W. A., *The Politics of Environmental Concern*,
        New York, Praeger, 1975.

1044.   Sive, M. R., ed., *Environmental Legislation*, New York,
        Praeger, 1976.

1045.   Spiro, T. G., *Environmental Science in Perspective*,
        New York, New York University Press, 1980.

1046.   Stewart, C. T., *Air Pollution, Human Health and Public
        Policy*, Lexington, MA, Lexington Books, 1979.

1047.   Tolley, G. S., *Environmental Policy*, Cambridge, MA,
        Ballinger, 1981.

1048. Whipple, W., *Planning of Water Quality Systems*, Lexing-
       ton, MA, Lexington Books, 1977.

1049. Wingo, L., and Evans, A., eds., *Public Economics and the
       Quality of Life*, Baltimore, MD, The Johns Hopkins Univer-
       sity Press, 1978.

G. Organization Theory and Behavior

Organization theory continues to ferment. Although
few instant classics were proclaimed in the last decade, many
significant works appeared accelerating the centrifugal
pressures in this area.

1050. Abrahamsson, B., *Bureaucracy or Participation*,
       Beverly Hills, CA, Sage, 1977.

1051. Aldrich, H. E., *Organizations and Environments*,
       Englewood Cliffs, NJ, Prentice-Hall, 1979.

1052. Argyris, C., *Intervention: Theory and Method*, Reading,
       MA, Addison-Wesley, 1970.

1053. Argyris, C., *Management and Organizational Development*,
       New York, McGraw-Hill, 1971.

1054. Bacharach, S. B., *Power and Politics in Organizations*,
       San Francisco, CA, Jossey-Bass, 1980.

1055. Bennis, W. G., *Beyond Bureaucracy*, New York, McGraw-Hill,
       1973.

1056. Blau, P. M., and Schoenherr, R. A., *The Structure of
       Organization*, New York, Basic Books, 1971.

1057. Brunner, R., and Brewer, G., *Organized Complexity*,
       New York, Free Press, 1971.

1058. Carroll, J. J., and Tosi, H. L., *MBO Applications and
       Research*, New York, Macmillan, 1973.

1059. Denhart, R. B., *In the Shadow of Organization*, Lawrence,
       KS, University of Kansas Press, 1981.

1060. Dessler, G., *Organization and Management*, Englewood
       Cliffs, NJ, Prentice-Hall, 1976.

1061. Dubin, R., *Theory Building*, New York, Free Press, 1978.

1062. Dubrin, A. J., *Casebook of Organizational Behavior*, New York, Pergamon, 1977.

1063. Edmunds, S., *Basics of Private and Public Management*, Lexington, MA, Lexington Books, 1978.

1064. French, W. L., and Bell, C. H., *Organization Development*, Englewood Cliffs, NJ, Prentice-Hall, 1973.

1065. Galbraith, J., *Designing Complex Organizations*, Reading, MA, Addison-Wesley, 1973.

1066. Golembiewski, R. T., *Renewing Organizations*, Itasca, IL, Peacock, 1972.

1067. Greiner, J. M., et al., *Productivity and Motivation*, Washington, DC, Urban Institute, 1981.

1068. Hage, J., and Aiken, M., *Social Change in Complex Organizations*, New York, Random House, 1970.

1069. Harmon, M. M., *Action Theory for Public Administration*, New York, Longman, 1981.

1070. Katz, D., et al., *Bureaucratic Encounters*, Ann Arbor, MI, University of Michigan Press, 1975.

1071. Kaufman, H., *The Limits of Organizational Change*, University, AL, University of Alabama Press, 1971.

1072. Khandwalla, P. N., *The Design of Organizations*, New York, Harcourt Brace Jovanovich, 1977.

1073. LaPorte, T. R., ed., *Organized Social Complexity*, Princeton, NJ, Princeton University Press, 1975.

1074. Levinson, H., *Organizational Diagnosis*, Cambridge, MA, Harvard University Press, 1972.

1075. Lippitt, G. L., *Organizational Renewal*, New York, Appleton-Century-Crofts, 1969.

1076. Luthans, F., *Organizational Behavior*, New York, McGraw-Hill, 1973.

1077. Margolies, N., and Wallace, J., *Organizational Change*, Glenview, IL, Scott, Foresman, 1973.

1078. Melcher, A. J., ed., *General Systems and Organization Theory*, Kent, OH, Kent State University Press, 1974.

1079. Perrow, C., *Organizational Analysis*, Belmont, CA, Wadsworth, 1970.

1080. Ramos, A. G., *The New Science of Organizations*, Toronto, Canada, University of Toronto Press, 1981.

1081. Tosi, H. L., and Hamner, W. C., eds., *Organizational Behavior and Management*, Chicago, St. Clair Press, 1977.

1082. Weinstein, D., *Bureaucratic Opposition*, New York, Pergamon Press, 1979.

1083. Wren, D. A., *The Evolution of Management Thought*, New York, Ronald Press, 1972.

1084. Zaltman, G., et al., *Innovations and Organizations*, New York, Wiley, 1973.

H. Public Finance

The crisis of public budgeting continues to capture attention, but other aspects of public finance also attracted significant research.

1085. Aaron, H. J., and Boskin, M. J., eds., *The Economics of Taxation*, Washington, DC, Brookings, 1978.

1086. Anderson, W. H., *Financing Modern Governments*, Boston, MA, Houghton Mifflin, 1973.

1087. Bahl, R., and Vogt, W., *Centralization and Tax Burdens*, Cambridge, MA, Ballinger, 1975.

1088. Balutis, A. P., and Butler, D. K., *The Political Purse-strings*, New York, Halstead Press, 1975.

1089. Bennett, R. J., *The Geography of Public Finance*, New York, Methuen, 1980.

1090. Blinder, A. S., et al., *The Economics of Public Finance*, Washington, DC, Brookings, 1974.

1091. Borcherding, T., ed., *Budgets and Bureaucrats*, Durham, NC, Duke University Press, 1977.

1092. Brundage, P. F., *The Bureau of the Budget*, New York, Praeger, 1970.

1093. Burkhead, J., and Miner, J., *Public Expenditure*, New York, Aldine, Atherton, 1971.

1094. Ferretti, F., *The Year The Big Apple Went Bust*, New York, Putnam, 1976.

1095. Fisher, L., *Presidential Spending Power*, Princeton, NJ, Princeton, University Press, 1975.

1096. Friedman, L. B., *Budgeting Municipal Expenditures*, New York, Praeger, 1975.

1097. Galbraith, J. K., *Economics and the Public Purpose*, Boston, MA, Houghton Mifflin, 1973.

1098. Haveman, R. H., *The Economics of the Public Sector*, New York, Wiley, 1970.

1099. Herber, B., *Modern Public Finance*, New York, Irwin, 1976.

1100. Leloup, L., *Budgetary Politics*, Brunswick, OH, Kings Court Communications, 1977.

1101. Meltsner, A., *The Politics of City Revenue*, Berkeley, CA, University of California Press, 1971.

1102. Oakes, W. E., ed., *The Political Economy of Fiscal Federalism*, Lexington, MA, Lexington Books, 1977.

1103. Ott, D. J., and Ott, A. F., *Federal Budget Policy*, Washington, DC, Brookings, 1977.

1104. Pfiffner, J. P., *The President, the Budget and Congress*, Boulder, CO, Westview, 1979.

1105. Shoup, C. E., *Public Finance*, Chicago, IL, Aldine, 1969.

1106. Stern, P., *The Rape of the Taxpayer*, New York, Random House, 1974.

1107. Wanat, J., *Introduction to Budgeting*, North Scituate, MA, Duxbury Press, 1978.

1108. Wholey, J. S., *Zero Base Budgeting and Program Evaluation*, Lexington, MA, D. C. Heath, 1978.

1109. Wildavsky, A., *Budgeting*, Boston, MA, Little, Brown, 1975.

I. Public Personnel Administration

The merit system has come under closer scrutiny and has been found wanting. Civil service reform is once again in the news while public sector labor relations continue to be of concern.

1110. Benokraitis, N. V., and Feagin, J. R., *Affirmative Action and Equal Opportunity*, Boulder, CO, Westview Press, 1978.

1111. Byers, K. T., ed., *Employee Training and Development in the Public Service*, Chicago, IL, International Public Management Association, 1970.

1112. Chapman, R. L., and Cleveland, F. N., *Meeting the Needs of Tommorrow's Public Service*, Washington, DC, National Academy of Public Administration, 1973.

1113. Gartner, A., et al., eds., *Public Service Employment*, New York, Praeger, 1973.

1114. Gershenfeld, W. J., et al., eds., *Scope of Public Sector Bargaining*, Lexington, MA, Lexington Books, 1977.

1115. Glazer, N., *Affirmative Discrimination*, New York, Basic Books, 1975.

1116. Harvey, D. R., *The Civil Service Commission*, New York, Praeger, 1969.

1117. Koch, J. V., and Chizmar, J. F., *The Economics of Affirmative Action*, Lexington, MA, D. C. Heath, 1976.

1118. Krislov, S., and Rosenbloom, D. H., *Representative Bureaucracy and the American Political System*, New York, Praeger, 1982.

1119.   Macy, J. W., *Public Service*, New York, Harper and Row, 1971.

1120.   Newland, C. A., et al., *MBO and Productivity Bargaining in the Public Service*, Chicago, IL, International Personnel Management Association, 1974.

1121.   Odiorne, G. S., *Personnel Administration by Objectives*, Homewood, IL, Irwin, 1971.

1122.   Pops, G. M., *Emergence of the Public Service Arbitrator*, Lexington, MA, D. C. Heath, 1976.

1123.   Rosenbloom, D. H., *Federal Equal Employment Opportunity*, New York, Praeger, 1977.

1124.   Saltstein, A., ed., *Public Employees and Policymaking*, Pacific Palisades, CA, Palisades Publishers, 1979.

1125.   Schick, R. P., and Couturier, J. J., *The Public Interest in Government Labor Relations*, Cambridge, MA, Ballinger, 1977.

1126.   Shafritz, J. M., *Position Classification*, New York, Praeger, 1973.

1127.   Telford, E., *The Principles of Public Personnel Administration*, Newark, DE, University of Delaware Press, 1976.

1128.   Weitzman, J., *The Scope of Bargaining in Public Employment*, New York, Praeger, 1975.

1129.   Zagoria, S., ed., *Public Workers and Public Unions*, Englewood Cliffs, NJ, Prentice-Hall, 1972.

J.   Public Policy and Regulation

The last decade has witnessed the emergence of public policy as a distinct discipline and profession in its own right. As a result, this area has probably experienced the most impressive growth.

1130.   Abert, J. G., and Kamrass, M., *Social Experiments and Social Program Evaluation*, Cambridge, MA, Ballinger, 1974.

1131. Amacher, R. C., et al., eds., *The Economic Approach to Public Policy*, Ithaca, NY, Cornell University Press, 1976.

1132. Art, R. J., *The TFX Decision*, Boston, MA, Little, Brown, 1968.

1133. Belshaw, C., *The Sorcerer's Apprentice*, New York, Pergamon Press, 1975.

1134. Breyer, S. G., *Regulation and Its Reform*, Cambridge, MA, Harvard University Press, 1982.

1135. Breyer, S. G., and MacAvoy, P., *Energy Regulation by the Federal Power Commission*, Washington, DC, Brookings, 1974.

1136. Brigham, J., ed., *Making Public Policy*, Lexington, MA, D. C. Heath, 1977.

1137. Brock, B., et al., *Public Policy Decision-Making*, New York, Harper and Row, 1973.

1138. Calabresi, G., and Bobbit, P., *Tragic Choices*, New York, Norton, 1978.

1139. Caputo, D. A., *Politics and Public Policy in America*, Philadelphia, PA, Lippincott, 1974.

1140. Culhane, P. J., *Public Lands Policy*, Baltimore, MD, Johns Hopkins Press, 1981.

1141. Dickson, P., *Think Tanks*, New York, Atheneum, 1971.

1142. Donovan, J. C., *The Policy Makers*, New York, Pegasus, 1970.

1143. Edwards, G. E., and Sharkansky, I., *The Policy Predicament*, San Francisco, CA, Freeman, 1978.

1144. Frohock, F. M., *Public Policy: Scope and Logic*, Englewood Cliffs, NJ, Prentice-Hall, 1979.

1145. Guttman, D., and Willner, B., *The Shadow Government*, New York, Pantheon, 1976.

1146. Hammond, K. R., ed., *Judgment and Decision in Public Policy Formation*, Boulder, CO, Westview Press, 1978.

1147. Hargrove, E. C., *The Missing Link*, Washington, DC,
       Urban Institute, 1975.

1148. Kelleher, G. J., ed., *The Challenge to Systems Analysis*,
       New York, Wiley, 1970.

1149. Lewin, A. Y., and Shakun, M. F., *Policy Sciences*,
       New York, Pergamon, 1974.

1150. Loehr, W., and Sandler, T., *Public Goods and Public
       Policy*, Beverly Hills, CA, Sage, 1978.

1151. Mack, R., *Planning on Uncertainty*, New York, Wiley,
       1970.

1152. Mosher, F. C., and Harr, J. E., *Programming Systems
       and Foreign Affairs Leadership*, New York, Oxford Uni-
       versity Press, 1979.

1153. Nachmias, D., *Public Policy Evaluation*, New York, St.
       Martin's Press, 1979.

1154. Poister, T. H., *Public Program Analysis*, Baltimore, MD,
       University Park Press, 1978.

1155. Rae, D. W., and Eismeier, T. J., eds., *Public Policy
       and Public Choice*, Beverly Hills, CA, Sage, 1979.

1156. Redford, E. S., *The Regulatory Process*, Austin, TX,
       University of Texas Press, 1969.

1157. Rose, R. S., *Public Choice and Public Policy*, Chicago,
       IL, Markham, 1971.

1158. Scioli, F., and Cook, T., eds., *Methodologies for Ana-
       lyzing Public Policies*, Lexington, MA, Lexington Books,
       1975.

1159. Siegel, R. L., and Weinberg, L. B., *Comparing Public
       Policies*, Homewood, IL, Dorsey, 1977.

1160. Sigler, J. A., *The Legal Sources of Public Policy*,
       Lexington, MA, Lexington Books, 1977.

1161. Tugwell, F., ed., *Search for Alternatives*, Cambridge,
       MA, Winthrop, 1973.

1162. Wade, L. L., and Curry, R. L., *A Logic of Public Policy*, Belmont, CA, Wadsworth, 1970.

1163. Zeckhauser, R., et al., *Benefit Cost and Policy Analysis*, Chicago, IL, Aldine, 1974.

K. Social Services/Health Care Administration

The welfare state continues to be an issue and a new respect for its beneficiaries has changed the terminology from social services to human resources or human services.

1164. Aiken, M., et al., *Coordinating Human Services*, San Francisco, CA, Jossey-Bass, 1975.

1165. Alford, R. R., *Health Care Politics*, Chicago, IL, University of Chicago Press, 1975.

1166. Atkinsson, C. C., et al., eds., *Evaluation of Human Services Programs*, New York, Academic Press, 1978.

1167. Ball, R. M., *Social Security*, New York, Columbia University Press, 1978.

1168. Brehm, H. P., *Medical Care for the Aged*, New York, Praeger, 1980.

1169. Brisbee, G. E., and Vraciu, R. A., eds., *Managing the Finances of Health Care Organizations*, Ann Arbor, MI, Health Administration Press, 1980.

1170. Campbell, R. R., *Social Security*, Stanford, CA, Hoover Institute Press, 1977.

1171. Davis, K., *National Health Insurance*, Washington, DC, Brookings, 1975.

1172. Derthick, M., *Uncontrollable Spending for Social Services Grants*, Washington, DC, Brookings, 1975.

1173. Donovan, J. C., *The Politics of Poverty*, Indianapolis, IN, Bobbs-Merrill, 1976.

1174. Furniss, N., and Tilton, T., *The Case for the Welfare State*, Bloomington, IN, Indiana University Press, 1977.

1175. Galper, J. H., *The Politics of Social Services*, Engle-
      wood Cliffs, NJ, Prentice-Hall, 1975.

1176. Goodwin, L., *Do The Poor Want to Work?*, Indianapolis,
      IN, Bobbs-Merrill, 1976.

1177. Janowitz, M., *Social Control of the Welfare State*,
      Chicago, IL, University of Chicago Press, 1976.

1178. Krefetz, S. P., *Welfare Policy Making and City Politics*,
      New York, Praeger, 1976.

1179. Levey, S., and Loomba, N. P., *Health Care Administration*,
      Philadelphia, PA, Lippincott, 1973.

1180. Levin, A., ed., *Regulating Health Care*, Philadelphia,
      PA, Academy of Political Science, 1980.

1181. Levitan, S. D., *The Greater Society's Poor Law*,
      Baltimore, MD, The Johns Hopkins University Press, 1969.

1182. Lindberg, D. A., *The Growth of Medical Information Sys-
      tems in the United States*, Lexington, MA, Lexington
      Books, 1979.

1183. Mandell, B. R., ed., *Welfare in America*, Englewood
      Cliffs, NJ, Prentice-Hall, 1975.

1184. Moynihan, D. P., *On Understanding Poverty*, New York,
      Basic Books, 1969.

1185. Moynihan, D. P., *The Politics of the Guaranteed Income*,
      New York, Random House, 1973.

1186. Plotnick, R. D., and Skidmore, F., *Progress Against
      Poverty*, New York, Academic Press, 1975.

1187. Stamps, P. L., *Evaluation of Outpatient Facilities*,
      Lexington, MA, Lexington Books, 1978.

1188. Steiner, R., *Managing the Human Service Organization*,
      Beverly Hills, CA, Sage, 1977.

1189. Vladeck, B. C., *Unloving Care*, New York, Basic Books,
      1980.

1190. Wilenski, H. L., *The Welfare State and Equality*,
      Berkeley, CA, University of California Press, 1975.

1191. Williams, W., *Social Policy Research and Analysis*,
       New York, American Elsevier, 1971.

1192. Williams, W., and Elmore, R., eds., *Social Program
       Implementation*, New York, Academic Press, 1976.

L.   Urban Administration

The reduction of urban violence in the last decade had
been accompanied by some diversion of academic attention from
urban problems. Nevertheless, the revitalization of American
cities remains a key issue.

1193. Appleyard, D., *Livable Streets*, Berkeley, University of
       California Press, 1981.

1194. Banovetz, J. J., ed., *Managing the Modern City*, Washington,
       DC, International City Management Association, 1971.

1195. Bent, A., and Rossum, R. A., eds., *Urban Administration*,
       Port Washington, NY, Kennikat Press, 1976.

1196. Bingham, R. D., *Public Housing and Urban Renewal*, New
       York, Praeger, 1975.

1197. Bish, R. L., *The Public Economy of Metropolitan Areas*,
       Chicago, Markham, 1971.

1198. Bish, R. L. and Ostrom, V., *Understanding Urban Government*,
       Indianapolis, Bobbs-Merrill, 1973.

1199. Boyer, B. D., *Cities Destroyed for Cash*, Chicago, Follett
       Publishing Co., 1973.

1200. Branch, M. C., *Continuous City Planning*, New York, Wiley,
       1981.

1201. Brewer, G. D., *Politicians, Bureaucrats and the Consultant*,
       New York, Basic Books, 1973.

1202. Brown, F. G., and Murphy, T. P., eds., *Emerging Patterns
       in Urban Administration*, Lexington, MA, Lexington Books,
       1970.

1203. Burchell, P. W., and Listokin, D., eds., *Cities Under
       Stress*, New Brunswick, NJ, Rutgers University, 1981.

1204. Caputo, D. A., and Cole, R. L., *Urban Politics and Decentralization*, Lexington, MA, Lexington Books, 1976.

1205. Cole, R. L., *Citizen Participation and the Urban Policy Process*, Lexington, MA, D. C. Heath, 1974.

1206. Daland, R. T., ed., *Comparative Urban Research*, Beverly Hills, CA, Sage, 1969.

1207. Forrester, J. W., *Urban Dynamics*, Cambridge, MA, MIT Press, 1969.

1208. Fox, D. M., *The Politics of City and State Bureaucracy*, Pacific Palisades, CA, Goodyear, 1974.

1209. Gorham, W., and Glazer, N., eds., *The Urban Predicament*, Washington, DC, Urban Institute, 1976.

1210. Hawley, W. D., and Rogers, D., *Improving Urban Management*, Beverly Hills, CA, Sage, 1976.

1211. Jackson, J. E., *Public Needs and Private Behavior in Metropolitan Areas*, Cambridge, MA, Ballinger, 1975.

1212. Levy, F. S., et al., *Urban Outcomes*, Berkeley, University of California Press, 1974.

1213. Lineberry, R. L., and Sharkansky, I., *Urban Politics and Public Policy*, New York, Harper and Row, 1978.

1214. Morgan, D. R., *Managing Urban America*, N. Scituate, MA, Duxbury Press, 1979.

1215. Murphy, T. P., and Warren, C. R., eds., *Organizing Public Services in Metropolitan America*, Lexington, MA, Lexington Books, 1974.

1216. Ostrom, E., ed., *The Delivery of Urban Services*, Beverly Hills, CA, Sage, 1976.

1217. Rosenbloom, R. S., and Russell, J. R., *New Tools in Urban Management*, Boston, Harvard Business School, 1971.

1218. Shipman, G. A., *Designing Program Action--Against Urban Poverty*, University, AL, University of Alabama Press, 1971.

1219. Stone, C. N., et al., *Urban Policy and Politics in a Bureaucratic Age*, Englewood Cliffs, NJ, Prentice-Hall, 1979

1220. Wilson, D. G., ed., *Handbook of Solid Waste Management*, New York, Van Nostrand, 1977.

INDEX OF ABSTRACTS, INDEXES, AND
CONTINUING BIBLIOGRAPHIES

Bibliographic sources listed in the Directory are indexed here
only under their latest title. Numbers after the title refer
to the item number and not to the page number.

INDEX OF JOURNALS

AUTHOR INDEX

Aaron, H. J., 706, 1085
Abert, J. G., 1130
Abrahamsson, B., 1050
Ackerman, B., 1021
Adelman, I., 987
Aiken, M., 1068, 1164
Aldrich, H. E., 1051
Alford, R. R., 1165
Alinsky, S. D., 707
Allan, P., 698
Allen, T. H., 708
Allensworth, D. T., 509
Allison, G. T., 709
Altschuler, A. A., 604, 632, 710
Amacher, R. C., 1131
Amick, G., 911
Anderson, F. R., 1022
Anderson, J., 927
Anderson, J. E., 516, 547, 581, 683
Anderson, S. V., 932
Anderson, W. H., 1086
Anton, T. J., 711
Appleby, P. H., 382, 394, 406
Appleyard, D., 1193
Argyris, C., 712, 713, 1052, 1053
Arnold, R. D., 933
Arrow, K. J., 714
Art, R. J., 1132
Ashford, D. E., 988
Atkinsson, C. C., 1166
Bacharach, S. B., 1054
Baden, J., 1033
Bahl, R., 1087

Baldwin, S., 526
Balk, W. L., 966
Ball, R. M., 1167
Balutis, A. P., 934, 1088
Banfield, E. C., 418, 609, 715
Banovetz, J. J., 1194
Bardach, E. C., 716
Barker, J. D., 935
Barkum, M., 1023
Barnard, C. I., 365
Barnett, H. G., 420
Bartholomew, P. C., 469, 488, 506
Barton, A. H., 659
Baruch, I., 373
Bauer, R. A., 598, 717
Beard, C. A., 374
Beauchamp, T. L., 912
Beck, J. M., 355
Becker, S. W., 967
Bell, C. H., 1064
Bell, D., 886
Bellone, C. J., 648
Belshaw, C., 1133
Beltrami, E. J., 968
Bennett, R. J., 1089
Bennis, W. G., 610, 718, 719, 720, 721, 1055
Benokraitis, N. V., 1110
Benson, G. C., 913
Bent, A., 1195
Benveniste, G., 989
Berg, L., 914
Berger, G., 936
Berger, R., 937
Berkley, G. E., 493, 517, 537, 570, 722

Marx, F. M., 387, 423, 451,
  467, 470
Maslow, A. H., 411
Matlack, W. F., 694
May, J. V., 644
Mayo, E., 357
Meadows, D., 1036
Medeiros, J. A., 534
Meier, K. J., 695
Melcher, A. J., 1078
Meltsner, A., 807, 1101
Merriam, C., 358
Merton, R. K., 408, 591
Meyer, M. W., 808
Meyerson, M., 418
Miewald, R., 541
Mikesell, J. L., 584
Milgram, S., 903
Miller, E. G., 607
Millett, J. D., 412, 461,
  471, 487
Milloy, R., 633
Mills, C. W., 389, 403
Miner, J., 1093
Montana, J., 970
Mooney, J. D., 368
Morgan, A. E., 1037
Morgan, D. R., 809
Morris, C. T., 987
Morrisey, G. T., 982
Morrow, W. L., 520, 564,
  954
Mosher, F. C., 492, 585, 626,
  630, 664, 676, 810, 811,
  812, 1152
Mosher, W. E., 363, 447, 450,
  455
Moynihan, D. P., 813, 1184,
  1185
Murin, W. J., 701
Murphy, J. T., 696
Murphy, T. P., 665, 955,
  1202, 1214
Musgrave, P. E., 814
Musgrave, R. A., 814
Musolf, L. D., 1007
Nachmias, D., 565, 1008,
  1153
Nader, R., 815
Nagel, S. S., 1038

Nakamura, R. T., 816
Nash, G. D., 678
Nathan, R. P., 817
Netzer, D., 818
Neuhauser, D., 967
Neustadt, R., 437
Newland, C. A., 653, 1120
Nielsen, W. A., 819
Nigro, F. A., 472, 482, 499,
  510, 525, 535, 566, 578,
  590
Nigro, L. G., 510, 525, 535,
  566, 578
Niskanen, W. A., 820
Nixson, F., 993
Nordland, W. J., 1039
Novick, D., 821
Novogrod, J., 679
Nystroom, P. C., 822
O'Connor, J., 823
O'Donnell, M. E., 601
O'Hara, P., 548
Oakes, W. E., 1102
Odiorne, G. S., 983, 1121
Ogul, M. S., 956
Okun, A. M., 824
Olson, D., 920
Olson, M., 825
Ophuls, W., 1040
Orlans, W., 654
Ostrom, E., 1215
Ostrom, V., 511, 1198
Ott, A. F., 1103
Ott, D. J., 1103
Paige, J. M., 1009
Palic, V. M., 687
Parsons, T., 390
Passel, P., 957
Payne, R., 926
Pearson, D., 927
Pechman, J. A., 826
Pennock, J., 904
Perelman, L. J., 1041
Perrow, C., 1079
Perry, J. L., 669
Peters, B. G., 542
Peters, C., 928
Peterson, J. E., 655
Petkas, P., 815